DATE DUE

APR 21 2007	
May 26 2007	
APR 29	

DEMCO, INC. 38-2931

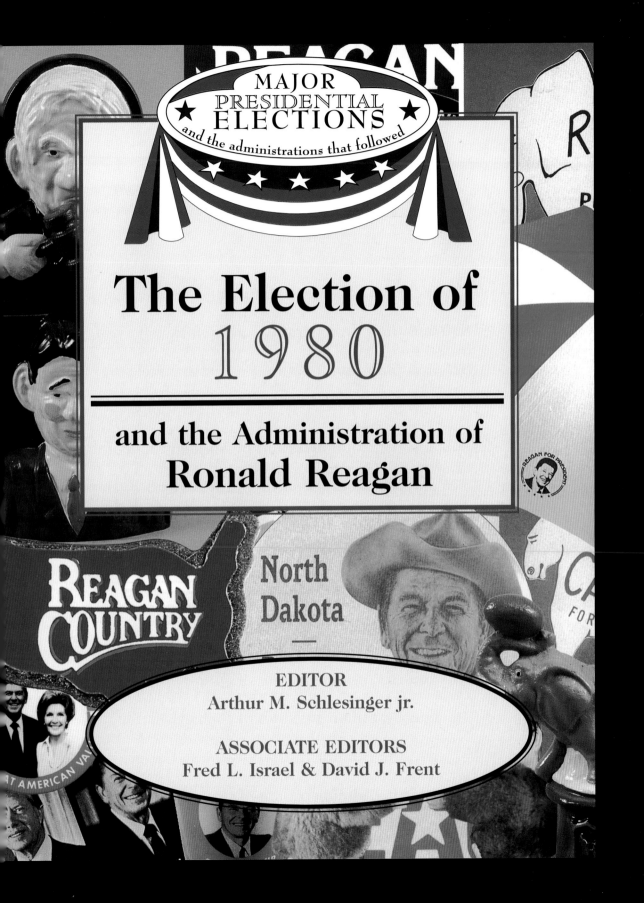

MAJOR PRESIDENTIAL ELECTIONS
and the administrations that followed

The Election of
1980

and the Administration of
Ronald Reagan

EDITOR
Arthur M. Schlesinger jr.

ASSOCIATE EDITORS
Fred L. Israel & David J. Frent

MAJOR
PRESIDENTIAL
ELECTIONS
and the administrations that followed

The Election of
1980

and the Administration of Ronald Reagan

EDITOR

Arthur M. Schlesinger, jr.
Albert Schweitzer Chair in the Humanities
The City University of New York

ASSOCIATE EDITORS

Fred L. Israel
Department of History
The City College of New York

David J. Frent
The David J. and Janice L. Frent
Political Americana Collection

Mason Crest Publishers
Philadelphia

Produced by OTTN Publishing, Stockton, New Jersey

Mason Crest Publishers
370 Reed Road
Broomall PA 19008
www.masoncrest.com

Research Consultant: Patrick R. Hilferty
Editorial Assistant: Jane Ziff

First printing

1 3 5 7 9 8 6 4 2

Library of Congress Cataloging-in-Publication Data

The election of 1980 and the administration of Ronald Reagan / editor, Arthur M. Schlesinger, Jr.; associate editors, Fred L. Israel & David J. Frent.
    p. cm. — (Major presidential elections and the administrations that followed)
Summary: A discussion of the presidential election of 1980 and the subsequent administration of Ronald Reagan, based on source documents.
   Includes bibliographical references and index.
   ISBN 1-59084-364-9
1. Presidents—United States—Election—1980—Juvenile literature. 2. Presidents—United States—Election—1980—Sources—Juvenile literature 3. Reagan, Ronald—Juvenile literature.
4. United States—Politics and government—1981-1989—Juvenile literature. 5. United States—Politics and government—1981-1989—Sources—Juvenile literature.
[1. Presidents—Election—1980—Sources. 2. Reagan, Ronald. 3. Elections. 4. United States—Politics and government—1981-1989—Sources.]
I. Schlesinger, Arthur Meier, 1917- II. Israel, Fred L. III. Frent, David J. IV. Series.
E875 .E44 2002
324.973'0926—dc21
                                           2002011772

★ **Publisher's note: all quotations in this book come from original sources, and contain the spelling and grammatical inconsistencies of the original text.** ★

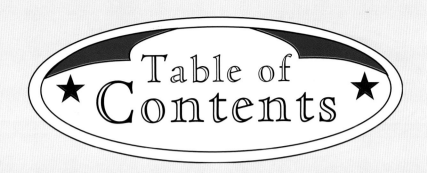

Table of Contents

★ INTRODUCTION ★
Arthur M. Schlesinger, Jr.

America suffers from a sort of intermittent fever—what one may call a quintan ague. Every fourth year there come terrible shakings, passing into the hot fit of the presidential election; then follows what physicians call "the interval"; then again the fit.

—James Bryce, *The American Commonwealth* (1888)

Running for president is the central rite in the American political order. It was not always so. *Choosing* the chief magistrate had been the point of the quadrennial election from the beginning, but it took a long while for candidates to *run* for the highest office in the land; that is, to solicit, visibly and actively, the support of the voters. These volumes show through text and illustration how those aspiring to the White House have moved on from ascetic self-restraint to shameless self-merchandising. This work thereby illuminates the changing ways the American people have conceived the role of their President. I hope it will also recall to new generations some of the more picturesque and endearing dimensions of American politics.

The primary force behind the revolution in campaign attitudes and techniques was a development unforeseen by the men who framed the Constitution—the rise of the party system. Party competition was not at all their original intent. Quite the contrary: inspired at one or two removes by Lord Bolingbroke's British tract of half a century earlier, *The Idea of a Patriot King*, the Founding Fathers envisaged a Patriot President, standing above party and faction, representing the whole people, offering the nation nonpartisan leadership virtuously dedicated to the common good.

The ideal of the Patriot President was endangered, the Founding Fathers believed, by twin menaces—factionalism and factionalism's ugly offspring, the demagogue. Party competition would only encourage unscrupulous men to appeal to popular passion and prejudice. Alexander Hamilton in the 71st Federalist bemoaned the plight of the people, "beset as they continually are . . . by the snares of the ambitious, the avaricious, the desperate, by the artifices of men who possess their confidence more than they deserve it, and of those who seek to possess rather than to deserve it."

Pervading the Federalist was a theme sounded explicitly both in the first paper and the last: the fear that unleashing popular passions would bring on "the military despotism of a victorious demagogue." If the "mischiefs of faction" were, James Madison admitted in the Tenth Federalist, "sown in the nature of man," the object of politics was to repress this insidious disposition, not to yield to it. "If I could not go to heaven but with a party," said Thomas Jefferson, "I would not go there at all."

So the Father of his Country in his Farewell Address solemnly warned his countrymen against "the baneful effects of the spirit of party." That spirit, Washington conceded, was "inseparable from our nature"; but for popular government it was "truly their worst enemy." The "alternate domination of one faction over another," Washington said, would lead in the end to "formal and permanent despotism." The spirit of a party, "a fire not to be quenched . . . demands a uniform vigilance to prevent its bursting into a flame, lest, instead of warming, it should consume."

Yet even as Washington called on Americans to "discourage and restrain" the spirit of party, parties were beginning to crystallize around him. The eruption of partisanship in defiance of such august counsel argued that party competition might well serve functional necessities in the democratic republic.

After all, honest disagreement over policy and principle called for candid debate. And parties, it appeared, had vital roles to play in the consummation of the Constitution. The distribution of powers among three equal branches inclined the national government toward a chronic condition of stalemate. Parties offered the means of overcoming the constitutional separation of powers by coordinating the executive and legislative branches and furnishing the connective tissue essential to effective government. As national associations, moreover, parties were a force against provincialism and separatism. As instruments of compromise, they encouraged, within the parties as well as between them, the containment and mediation of national quarrels, at least until slavery broke the parties up. Henry D. Thoreau cared little enough for politics, but he saw the point: "Politics is, as it were, the gizzard of society, full of grit and gravel, and the two political parties are its two opposite halves, which grind on each other."

Furthermore, as the illustrations in these volumes so gloriously remind us, party competition was a great source of entertainment and fun—all the more important in those faraway days before the advent of baseball and football, of movies and radio and television. "To take a hand in the regulation of society and to discuss it," Alexis de Tocqueville observed when he visited America in the 1830s, "is his biggest concern and, so to speak, the only pleasure an American knows. . . . Even the women frequently attend public meetings and listen to political harangues as a recreation from their household labors. Debating clubs are, to a certain extent, a substitute for theatrical entertainments."

Condemned by the Founding Fathers, unknown to the Constitution, parties nonetheless imperiously forced themselves into political life. But the party system rose from the bottom up. For half a century, the first half-dozen Presidents continued to hold themselves above party. The disappearance of the Federalist Party after the War of 1812 suspended party competition. James Monroe, with no opponent at all in the election of 1820, presided proudly over the Era of Good Feelings, so called because there were no parties around to excite ill feelings. Monroe's successor, John Quincy Adams, despised electioneering and inveighed against the "fashion of peddling for popularity by

traveling around the country gathering crowds together, hawking for public dinners, and spouting empty speeches." Men of the old republic believed presidential candidates should be men who already deserved the people's confidence rather than those seeking to win it. Character and virtue, not charisma and ambition, should be the grounds for choosing a President.

Adams was the last of the old school. Andrew Jackson, by beating him in the 1828 election, legitimized party politics and opened a new political era. The rationale of the new school was provided by Jackson's counselor and successor, Martin Van Buren, the classic philosopher of the role of party in the American democracy. By the time Van Buren took his own oath of office in 1837, parties were entrenched as the instruments of American self-government. In Van Buren's words, party battles "rouse the sluggish to exertion, give increased energy to the most active intellect, excite a salutary vigilance over our public functionaries, and prevent that apathy which has proved the ruin of Republics."

Apathy may indeed have proved the ruin of republics, but rousing the sluggish to exertion proved, ironically, the ruin of Van Buren. The architect of the party system became the first casualty of the razzle-dazzle campaigning the system quickly generated. The Whigs' Tippecanoe-and-Tyler-too campaign of 1840 transmuted the democratic Van Buren into a gilded aristocrat and assured his defeat at the polls. The "peddling for popularity" John Quincy Adams had deplored now became standard for party campaigners.

But the new methods were still forbidden to the presidential candidates themselves. The feeling lingered from earlier days that stumping the country in search of votes was demagoguery beneath the dignity of the presidency. Van Buren's code permitted—indeed expected—parties to inscribe their creed in platforms and candidates to declare their principles in letters published in newspapers. Occasionally candidates—William Henry Harrison in 1840, Winfield Scott in 1852—made a speech, but party surrogates did most of the hard work.

As late as 1858, Van Buren, advising his son John, one of the great popular orators of the time, on the best way to make it to the White House, emphasized the "rule . . . that the people will never make a man President who is so importunate as to show by his life and conversation that he not only has an eye on, but is in active pursuit of the office. . . . No man who has laid himself out for it, and was unwise enough to let the people into his secret, ever yet obtained it. Clay, Calhoun, Webster, Scott, and a host of lesser lights, should serve as a guide-post to future aspirants."

The continuing constraint on personal campaigning by candidates was reinforced by the desire of party managers to present their nominees as all things to all men. In 1835 Nicholas Biddle, the wealthy Philadelphian who had been Jackson's mortal opponent in the famous Bank War, advised the Whigs not to let General Harrison "say one single word about his principles or his creed. . . . Let him say nothing, promise nothing. Let no committee, no convention, no town meeting ever extract from him a single word about what he thinks now, or what he will do hereafter. Let the use of pen and ink be wholly forbidden as if he were a mad poet in Bedlam."

We cherish the memory of the famous debates in 1858 between Abraham Lincoln and Stephen A. Douglas. But those debates were not part of a presidential election. When the presidency was at stake two years later, Lincoln gave no campaign speeches on the issues darkly dividing the country. He even expressed doubt about party platforms—"the formal written platform system," as he called it. The candidate's character and record, Lincoln thought, should constitute his platform: "On just such platforms all our earlier and better Presidents were elected."

However, Douglas, Lincoln's leading opponent in 1860, foreshadowed the future when he broke the sound barrier and dared venture forth on thinly disguised campaign tours. Yet Douglas established no immediate precedent. Indeed, half a dozen years later Lincoln's successor, Andrew Johnson, discredited presidential stumping by his "swing around the circle" in the midterm

election of 1866. "His performances in a western tour in advocacy of his own election," commented Benjamin F. Butler, who later led the fight in Congress for Johnson's impeachment, ". . . disgusted everybody." The tenth article of impeachment charged Johnson with bringing "the high office of the President of the United States into contempt, ridicule, and disgrace" by delivering "with a loud voice certain intemperate, inflammatory, and scandalous harangues . . . peculiarly indecent and unbecoming in the Chief Magistrate of the United States."

Though presidential candidates Horatio Seymour in 1868, Rutherford B. Hayes in 1876, and James A. Garfield in 1880 made occasional speeches, only Horace Greeley in 1872, James G. Blaine in 1884, and most spectacularly, William Jennings Bryan in 1896 followed Douglas's audacious example of stumping the country. Such tactics continued to provoke disapproval. Bryan, said John Hay, who had been Lincoln's private secretary and was soon to become McKinley's secretary of state, "is begging for the presidency as a tramp might beg for a pie."

Respectable opinion still preferred the "front porch" campaign, employed by Garfield, by Benjamin Harrison in 1888, and most notably by McKinley in 1896. Here candidates received and addressed numerous delegations at their own homes—a form, as the historian Gil Troy writes, of "stumping in place."

While candidates generally continued to stand on their dignity, popular campaigning in presidential elections flourished in these years, attaining new heights of participation (82 percent of eligible voters in 1876 and never once from 1860 to 1900 under 70 percent) and new wonders of pyrotechnics and ballyhoo. Parties mobilized the electorate as never before, and political iconography was never more ingenious and fantastic. "Politics, considered not as the science of government, but as the art of winning elections and securing office," wrote the keen British observer James Bryce, "has reached in the United States a development surpassing in elaborateness that of England or France as much as the methods of those countries surpass the methods of

Servia or Roumania." Bryce marveled at the "military discipline" of the parties, at "the demonstrations, the parades and receptions, the badges and brass bands and triumphal arches," at the excitement stirred by elections— and at "the disproportion that strikes a European between the merits of the presidential candidate and the blazing enthusiasm which he evokes."

Still the old taboo held back the presidential candidates themselves. Even so irrepressible a campaigner as President Theodore Roosevelt felt obliged to hold his tongue when he ran for reelection in 1904. This unwonted abstinence reminded him, he wrote in considerable frustration, of the July day in 1898 when he was "lying still under shell fire" during the Spanish-American War. "I have continually wished that I could be on the stump myself."

No such constraint inhibited TR, however, when he ran again for the presidency in 1912. Meanwhile, and for the first time, *both* candidates in 1908—Bryan again, and William Howard Taft—actively campaigned for the prize. The duties of the office, on top of the new requirements of campaigning, led Woodrow Wilson to reflect that same year, four years before he himself ran for President, "Men of ordinary physique and discretion cannot be Presidents and live, if the strain be not somehow relieved. We shall be obliged always to be picking our chief magistrates from among wise and prudent athletes,—a small class."

Theodore Roosevelt and Woodrow Wilson combined to legitimate a new conception of presidential candidates as active molders of public opinion in active pursuit of the highest office. Once in the White House, Wilson revived the custom, abandoned by Jefferson, of delivering annual state of the union addresses to Congress in person. In 1916 he became the first incumbent President to stump for his own reelection.

The activist candidate and the bully-pulpit presidency were expressions of the growing democratization of politics. New forms of communication were reconfiguring presidential campaigns. In the nineteenth century the press, far more fiercely partisan then than today, had been the main carrier of political

information. In the twentieth century the spread of advertising techniques and the rise of the electronic media—radio, television, computerized public opinion polling—wrought drastic changes in the methodology of politics. In particular the electronic age diminished and now threatens to dissolve the historic role of the party.

The old system had three tiers: the politician at one end; the voter at the other; and the party in between. The party's function was to negotiate between the politician and the voters, interpreting each to the other and providing the link that held the political process together. The electric revolution has substantially abolished the sovereignty of the party. Where once the voter turned to the local party leader to find out whom to support, now he looks at television and makes up his own mind. Where once the politician turned to the local party leader to find out what people are thinking, he now takes a computerized poll.

The electronic era has created a new breed of professional consultants, "handlers," who by the 1980s had taken control of campaigns away from the politicians. The traditional pageantry—rallies, torchlight processions, volunteers, leaflets, billboards, bumper stickers—is now largely a thing of the past. Television replaces the party as the means of mobilizing the voter. And as the party is left to wither on the vine, the presidential candidate becomes more pivotal than ever. We shall see the rise of personalist movements, founded not on historic organizations but on compelling personalities, private fortunes, and popular frustrations. Without the stabilizing influence of parties, American politics would grow angrier, wilder, and more irresponsible.

Things have changed considerably from the austerities of the old republic. Where once voters preferred to call presumably reluctant candidates to the duties of the supreme magistracy and rejected pursuit of the office as evidence of dangerous ambition, now they expect candidates to come to them, explain their views and plead for their support. Where nonpartisan virtue had been the essence, now candidates must prove to voters that they have the requisite

"fire in the belly." "'Twud be inth'restin," said Mr. Dooley, ". . . if th' fathers iv th' counthry cud come back an' see what has happened while they've been away. In times past whin ye voted f'r prisident ye didn't vote f'r a man. Ye voted f'r a kind iv a statue that ye'd put up in ye'er own mind on a marble pidistal. Ye nivir heerd iv George Wash'nton goin' around th' counthry distributin' five cint see-gars."

We have reversed the original notion that ambition must be disguised and the office seek the man. Now the man—and soon, one must hope, the woman— seeks the office and does so without guilt or shame or inhibition. This is not necessarily a degradation of democracy. Dropping the disguise is a gain for candor, and personal avowals of convictions and policies may elevate and educate the electorate.

On the other hand, the electronic era has dismally reduced both the intellectual content of campaigns and the attention span of audiences. In the nineteenth century political speeches lasted for a couple of hours and dealt with issues in systematic and exhaustive fashion. Voters drove wagons for miles to hear Webster and Clay, Bryan and Teddy Roosevelt, and felt cheated if the famous orator did not give them their money's worth. Then radio came along and cut political addresses down first to an hour, soon to thirty minutes—still enough time to develop substantive arguments.

But television has shrunk the political talk first to fifteen minutes, now to the sound bite and the thirty-second spot. Advertising agencies today sell candidates with all the cynical contrivance they previously devoted to selling detergents and mouthwash. The result is the debasement of American politics. "The idea that you can merchandise candidates for high office like breakfast cereal," Adlai Stevenson said in 1952, "is the ultimate indignity to the democratic process."

Still Bryce's "intermittent fever" will be upon us every fourth year. We will continue to watch wise if not always prudent athletes in their sprint for the White House, enjoy the quadrennial spectacle and agonize about the outcome.

"The strife of the election," said Lincoln after his reelection in 1864, "is but human-nature practically applied to the facts. What has occurred in this case, must ever recur in similar cases. Human-nature will not change."

Lincoln, as usual, was right. Despite the transformation in political methods there remains a basic continuity in political emotions. "For a long while before the appointed time has come," Tocqueville wrote more than a century and a half ago, "the election becomes the important and, so to speak, the all-engrossing topic of discussion. Factional ardor is redoubled, and all the artificial passions which the imagination can create in a happy and peaceful land are agitated and brought to light. . . .

"As the election draws near, the activity of intrigue and the agitation of the populace increase; the citizens are divided into hostile camps, each of which assumes the name of its favorite candidate; the whole nation glows with feverish excitement; the election is the daily theme of the press, the subject of every private conversation, the end of every thought and every action, the sole interest of the present.

"It is true," Tocqueville added, "that as soon as the choice is determined, this ardor is dispelled, calm returns, and the river, which had nearly broken its banks, sinks to its usual level; but who can refrain from astonishment that such a storm should have arisen?"

The election storm in the end blows fresh and clean. With the tragic exception of 1860, the American people have invariably accepted the result and given the victor their hopes and blessings. For all its flaws and follies, democracy abides.

Let us now turn the pages and watch the gaudy parade of American presidential politics pass by in all its careless glory.

The Election
of 1980

Jules Witcover is a syndicated political columnist and the author of numerous books on politics, including *The Trivial Pursuit of the Presidency, 1988* (1989); *Revolt at the Ballot Box, 1992* (1993); and *No Way to Pick a President, 2000* (2001).

y 1980, the development of a cadre of career campaign managers, consultants, poll-takers, fund-raisers and media experts had reached full flower in presidential politics. These political technocrats had by now largely replaced the amateur advisers and professional politicians of old drawn to a presidential campaign essentially by personal association with the candidate or by party loyalty. The new breed was motivated not so much by friendship or party, or even ideology, as by a desire to build personal influence and personal wealth through the dispensing—and sale, at high rates—of their professional services.

These "hired guns," as they came to be called, looked upon the candidate who employed them in much the same way that a manufacturer looks upon a product he makes and then seeks to sell to the largest possible market. The basic approach had been evident in politics for a long time, particularly at the local and state levels in trendsetting states like California, but it had reached its most conspicuous implementation in the 1968 presidential campaign of Richard Nixon. Having lost one presidential race in 1960 despite campaigning at an exhausting pace, Nixon and his advisors set out in 1968 to analyze the challenge in terms of the new television era, as no campaigners had done before.

A former advertising executive, H. R. Haldeman, was a leading figure in masterminding a Nixon campaign sharply curtailing the traditional dawn-to-dusk retail campaigning that exposed the candidate to relatively few voters but to endless physical strain. While Nixon's Democratic foe, Hubert H. Humphrey, by tradition and by personal style slogged determinedly through eighteen-hour campaign days, Republican Nixon ran a much more disciplined, leisurely campaign designed by his professional advisers for maximum television exposure.

Each day by noon, Nixon would deliver one well-executed speech at or near a major airport from which film of his appearance could be whisked back to New York (these were pre-satellite days) in time for the network evening news shows. Then he would often disappear from public view, while aides fed "position papers" to the accompanying press. Humphrey meanwhile would make numerous appearances, with the networks capturing on film his best and worst performances, often using the worst. Then, observing "balance," they would use the only film of Nixon they had. In this way political technocrats managed through most of the campaign to put their candidate's best foot forward.

In ensuing presidential elections, the Republicans particularly learned from the 1968 Nixon example and conducted controlled campaigns in the hands of professionals. The Democrats, meanwhile, more often than not campaigned in the traditional all-out fashion, with a mix of amateurs and professionals. The Nixon pros easily won again in 1972, their manipulations and abuses of the electoral process in the Watergate scandal not fully realized by voters at the time. And in 1976, the "hired guns" laboring for President Gerald R. Ford came within an eyelash of beating the "amateur hour" team of Georgia-based political newcomers working for Democrat Jimmy Carter. The skills of the Ford pros made a race of it despite Ford's politically disastrous pardon of Nixon in the wake of the Watergate reve-

Ronald Reagan was elected governor of California in 1966 and reelected in 1970.

The Republican Party entered the 1980 campaign with confidence. The clear choice of the rank and file was 69-year-old Ronald Reagan. As governor of California for eight years, Reagan became the nation's best-known Republican politician because he associated himself with virtually every conservative cause.

Movie lobby card. *Hellcats of the Navy* (1957) was the only movie in which Reagan and Nancy Davis, his wife-to-be, appeared together.

lations that had driven Nixon from the presidency and elevated Ford to it.

In that 1976 campaign, Ford first withstood a serious challenge for the Republican nomination from Governor Ronald Reagan of California, who had assembled a team of some of the best young career political operatives, led by John Sears, a former Nixon law firm associate and political aide. After Ford's defeat by Carter, the Reagan team reassembled under Sears' direction and began planning for 1980. Sears believed he had the perfect candidate for the television era—a former movie actor accustomed to taking direction. The stage was set, or so Sears thought, for the classic television-age presidential campaign, featuring the communications skills of a professional actor playing a role created for him by professional directors who knew as a result of their research and political experience what it would take to win.

At the same time, the incumbent president, Jimmy Carter, again turned to the friends and associates from Georgia, together with a few professionals with national presidential campaign experience, to help win

A selection of Reagan campaign buttons. Invariably smiling, the 69-year-old candidate was projected as a virile westerner.

N.J. CITIZENS FOR

TOGETHER A NEW BEGINNING

LET'S MAKE AMERICA GREAT AGAIN

1980

Reagan President   Bush Vice President

LEADERSHIP FOR THE 80'S

REAGAN COUNTRY

REAGAN COUNTRY

KANSANS 1980 REAGAN

MAKE AMERICA GREAT AGAIN

North Dakota — Reagan Country

re-election against the survivor of the Republican primaries. Six other Republicans vied with Reagan for their party's nomination: former congressman, United Nations ambassador, and CIA director George Bush; Senator Howard H. Baker of Tennessee and Senator Bob Dole of Kansas; former Secretary of Treasury John B. Connally; and representatives John Anderson and Philip Crane of Illinois. Carter as the incumbent Democrat was challenged by Senator Edward M. Kennedy of Massachusetts and Governor Edmund G. (Jerry) Brown Jr. of California.

All candidates in both parties had their "hired guns," but a phenomenon was already emerging that marked a clear difference in the two parties and was to have an increasingly important effect on their relative success in presidential elections. While the Democrats continued to depend on a mix of amateurs and professionals attracted to the candidate, the Republicans were well on their way to building a durable stable of political technocrats.

In the familiar if overworked parlance of horseracing in politics, Democrats more often than not were one-horse jockeys, signing up for a particular presidential campaign out of personal devotion to or belief in a single candidate. If that candidate lost, as Democrats were developing the habit of doing during this period (they elected only one of their own, Carter in 1976, over a period of six presidential elections through 1988), most of his campaign workers would go back to their private pursuits. Also, Democrats whose candidate failed to win the party nomination would customarily go home rather than sign on with the winner—often because the nominee did not ask them.

Republican operatives, by contrast, were more committed to the horse race than they were to the one horse they were riding in the primary elections. If their candidate lost the nomination, most of them stood ready to help the winner—and were asked to help by the Republican nominee. After the general election, win or lose, these Republican political technicians

Re-Elect
Carter-
Mondale

A Tested and Trustworthy Team.

Poster for Carter and Mondale. This was the standard Democratic campaign poster.

would be "warehoused" in well-paying positions with the national or state party committees or in Washington law, lobbying, and political consulting firms, against the time they would be needed for the next presidential campaign. For example, the man who managed the Ford campaign in 1976, James A. Baker III, in 1980 signed on as manager of the George Bush campaign. After Bush lost the nomination to Reagan, Baker accepted the assignment of negotiating the conditions of Reagan's television debates with Carter.

This distinction between Republicans and Democrats concerning the use and dominance of political technocrats was pronounced in the campaign of 1980. On the Democratic side, the contrast essentially was between the incumbent and his severest critic within the party, Kennedy, who saw Carter as indecisive and uncaring in a nation where the needs of the traditional Democratic constituencies—the poor, the blue-collar workers, and racial and ethnic minorities—were being neglected. The Carter-Kennedy competition took on a personal bitterness and although Carter disposed of Kennedy and Brown without undue difficulty, that personal bitterness extended to the staffs and supporters of both men. By the time Carter had won renomination by turning back an effort by the Kennedy camp to break Carter's hold on pledged delegates at the national convention, the chances of reconciliation for the general-election campaign were shattered. The Kennedy people went home and sulked, and Carter—faced with widespread public dissatisfaction with his leadership—was left to wage his reelection campaign largely with the team that had narrowly won the presidency for him in 1976.

On the Republican side, Reagan at first encountered equally contentious opposition from the field of six challengers. But he was able to ride out that early adversity with a minimum of intra-party bitterness, and to recruit for the fall campaign many of the political professionals who had labored for the losers (except for supporters of

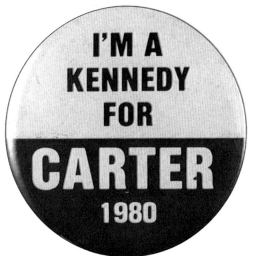

Celluloid button for Carter.
Senator Edward "Ted" Kennedy of Massachusetts challenged Carter for the 1980 Democratic nomination. His primary campaign seemed disorganized and unfocused. He could not adequately articulate why he wanted to be president. Above all, he could not explain an automobile accident in 1969 on the island of Chappaquiddick in Massachusetts in which a young woman was killed.

Novelty dolls of Reagan and Bush.

Anderson, who persevered as a third-party candidate). The only real scare for Reagan came in the year's first precinct caucuses in Iowa, where Reagan (on Sears's advice largely) left the campaign to his hired guns and they miscalculated, enabling Bush to upset him there.

In advance of the caucuses, Sears had estimated on the basis of past turnouts how many voters would have to be produced at the small neighborhood meetings across the state on caucus night to win. He set his professional organizers to work and held his popular candidate out of the state until the final weekend, assuming he could keep him above the fray while the other six contenders in frustration went after each other. Bush, however, had his own professional—a young organizer named Rich Bond who quietly put together his own network of supporters. The Bush team blindsided Reagan by swelling the traditional caucus-night turnout on which Sears had made his calculations, producing about three thousand more votes for Bush than Sears mustered for Reagan.

Overnight, Reagan fell from front-runner to question mark. In the next test, the New Hampshire primary, he was obliged to return to intensive street campaigning, dispensing his personal charm and appealing rhetoric about getting government "off the backs" of average voters. By doing so,

★ ★ ★ ★ ★   ★ ★ ★ ★ ★

QUAYLE   REAGAN   ORR

VOTE FOR
THE REPUBLICAN TEAM
FOR THE '80's
PULL LEVER 'A'

SUESS   MUTZ

Indiana campaign card for Reagan. Dan Quayle successfully ran for the Senate.

Quayle, a young lawyer and newspaperman from Indiana, defeated a Democratic incumbent in a congressional race in 1976, the same year his party lost the presidency. Two years later, at age thirty-one, Quayle unseated the distinguished Democratic Senator Birch Bayh. Quayle was overwhelming re-elected for a second term in 1984. In 1988, Republican nominee George H. W. Bush chose Quayle to be his vice presidential candidate. Quayle held that office from 1989 to 1993.

Reagan rapidly restored himself as the candidate to beat, capping his comeback with a clever bit of stage managing by Sears that ended Bush's brief "Big Mo" (for momentum, as the buoyant Bush liked to call the windfall from his Iowa upset). In a debate scheduled to be a two-man affair between Reagan and Bush, Sears on Reagan's behalf invited the other candidates to take part. When they appeared on the platform, Reagan

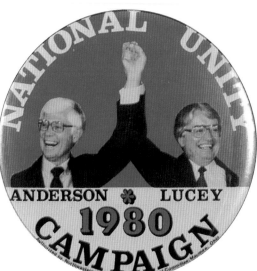

Representative John Anderson and Wisconsin governor Patrick Lucey, both liberal Republicans, ran on a third-party ticket. Anderson called it a "National Unity" campaign. They received 5.5 million votes.

demanded that they be seated, as Bush sat stonily and unwaveringly by. The other candidates, thus rebuffed, finally left, but Reagan came off as the hero and good sport, Bush as the villain and grouch, and Bush never recovered.

In spite of the dramatic turnaround for Reagan in New Hampshire, he fired Sears and two of his best professional associates, Charles Black and James Lake, in an internal squabble and brought in as his campaign manager New York lawyer William J. Casey, a heavy-handed former intelligence official of conspiratorial nature and suspicions. The Reagan campaign by now, however, had been set on its winning course and the candidate himself, by force of his personality and appealing (if simplistic) anti-government message, assumed the dominant role. In the remaining primary contests and in television commercials that gave voters their main exposure to him, Reagan was the featured player reciting his familiar script flawlessly.

By the time of the Republican National Convention in Detroit, the only question of much interest was Reagan's choice of a running mate. Bush seemed an obvious choice by nature of his second-place finish in the contest for delegates, but Reagan was unable to shake the highly unfavorable impression Bush's unbending behavior had left on him in the New Hampshire debate fiasco. So when one of his "hired guns," pollster Richard Wirthlin, reported surveys indicating that the strongest running mate would be the man who had beaten Reagan for the 1976 nomination—Gerald Ford—Reagan listened. With Bush the most obvious alternative, Reagan was not disposed to dismiss out of hand the notion that a former

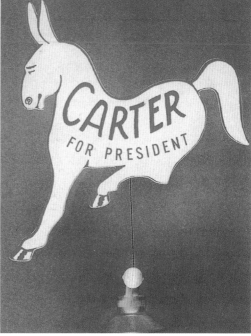

Suction cup novelties for Reagan and Carter.

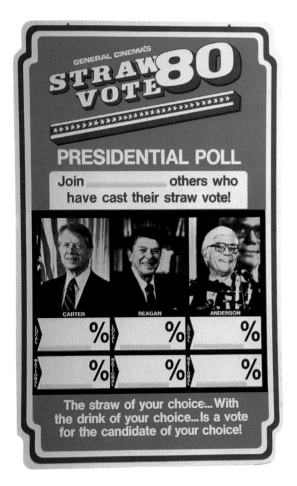

"Straw vote" slate issued by General Cinema Company for movie refreshment stands.

President might consider accepting the number two job he already once held.

There then took place at the convention a brief but fascinating circus that underscored the role that network television had come to play in the presidential-election process. As purely exploratory talks were between Reagan and Ford advisers on the possibility of a Reagan-Ford "dream ticket," and then between the principals themselves, Ford agreed to a live interview with CBS News anchorman Walter Cronkite. Talk of the "dream ticket" had now reached the convention floor and when Cronkite asked Ford about it, the former President proceeded to set out the conditions that would have to be met if he were to accept. And when Cronkite cast Ford's view of the job as "something like a co-presidency," Ford did not demur. In a flash, the idea was sweeping through the convention—causing great consternation among Reagan advisers who began to wonder what might be given away in this bizarre striving for the strongest possible Republican ticket. Finally, by mutual acquiescence, the notion was abandoned, and Reagan somewhat reluctantly agreed to accept Bush as his running mate.

The Democrats, meanwhile, were discovering that for all the growing dominance of political technicians in presidential politics, all the master-minding by them based on their poll-taking, and all the slickness of their television advertising, events still could be controlling. The events that unfolded in 1979 and early 1980 worked heavily in favor of Jimmy Carter in his successful pursuit of renomination, but they then posed insur-mountable barriers to his reelection in the fall campaign.

The first of these was the seizing of the American embassy in Iran in November 1979 and the eventual detention of fifty-two American hostages in protest against a decision to permit the deposed shah of Iran to enter the United States for emergency cancer treatment. Carter immediately focused on the hostage crisis and was preoccupied with it in December when Soviet troops suddenly invaded Afghanistan. Kennedy was already campaigning against

A selection of Carter-Mondale campaign buttons.

Carter in Iowa and a televised debate had been scheduled there, also to include Brown. But Carter seized on the foreign policy crises as reasons to pull out of the debate and withdraw to a "Rose Garden strategy" for re-nomination.

Without the incumbent on the hustings offering a target, Kennedy and Brown could not get their campaigns off the ground. Kennedy already was struggling as a result of another episode that had demonstrated television's increasing influence in presidential campaigns. In a hard-hitting interview with Roger Mudd, then of CBS News, Kennedy had been unable to provide a lucid and persuasive answer to the most obvious question for which any White House aspirant should be prepared: "Why do you want to be President?" He stammered and wandered through one of political television's most embarrassing moments for a candidate and never fully recovered, although he did run a more credible campaign once Carter, as a result of another event, abandoned his Rose Garden strategy.

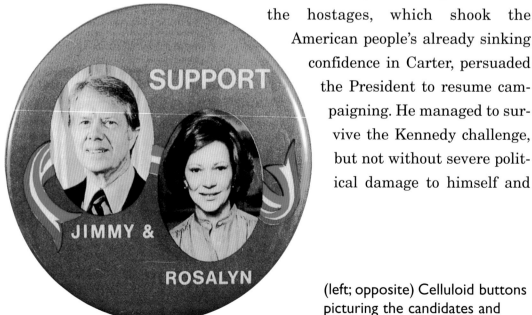

A botched attempt in late April to rescue the hostages, which shook the American people's already sinking confidence in Carter, persuaded the President to resume campaigning. He managed to survive the Kennedy challenge, but not without severe political damage to himself and

(left; opposite) Celluloid buttons picturing the candidates and their wives.

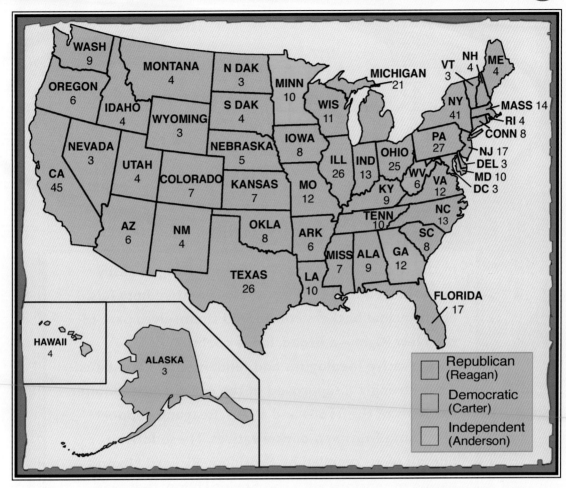

WASH 9
MONTANA 4
N DAK 3
MINN 10
MICHIGAN 21
VT 3
NH 4
ME 4
OREGON 6
IDAHO 4
S DAK 4
WIS 11
NY 41
MASS 14
WYOMING 3
IOWA 8
PA 27
RI 4
CONN 8
NEVADA 3
UTAH 4
NEBRASKA 5
ILL 26
IND 13
OHIO 25
NJ 17
CA 45
COLORADO 7
KANSAS 7
MO 12
KY 9
WV 6
VA 12
DEL 3
MD 10
DC 3
AZ 6
NM 4
OKLA 8
ARK 6
TENN 10
NC 13
SC 8
TEXAS 26
LA 10
MISS 7
ALA 9
GA 12
FLORIDA 17
HAWAII 4
ALASKA 3

☐ Republican (Reagan)

☐ Democratic (Carter)

☐ Independent (Anderson)

"Ask yourself, are you better off than you were four years ago?" Ronald Reagan asked voters during the 1980 presidential campaign. They answered by giving him a resounding victory on Election Day. Reagan won 50.7 percent of the popular vote (the incumbent president, Jimmy Carter, received 41 percent of the vote and John Anderson finished a relatively strong third-party campaign with 6.6 percent of the vote). Reagan easily won a majority in the electoral college, 489 to 49.

Reagan Accepts the Nomination

In the Republican primaries, Ronald Reagan easily outdistanced a host of other conservative hopefuls. His principal backers considered themselves part of the New Right—a broad, loose coalition of conservative ideologues and fundamental Christians. They strongly disapproved of the social and economic excesses of the 1960s and 1970s. Reagan's support also came from neo-conservatives. These former liberals were repelled by President Richard Nixon's easing of tensions with the Soviet Union, that was continued by the Ford and Carter administrations. They charged that the United States had allowed the Soviets to become a dangerous adversary which now had superiority in both conventional and nuclear arms. This superiority had encouraged the Soviets to engage in reckless adventures such as their support of worldwide terrorism and their 1979 invasion of Afghanistan. Reagan was nominated on the first ballot. He chose George H. Bush, former head of the Central Intelligence Agency, as his running mate.

We are awed—and rightly so—by the forces of destruction at loose in the world in this nuclear era.

But neither can we be naive or foolish. Four times in my lifetime America has gone to war, bleeding the lives of its young men into the sands of island beachheads, the fields of Europe and the jungles and rice paddies of Asia. We know only too well that war comes not when the forces of freedom are strong, it is when they are weak that tyrants are tempted.

We simply cannot learn these lessons the hard way again without risking our destruction.

Of all the objectives we seek, first and foremost is the establishment of lasting world peace. We must always stand ready to negotiate in good faith, ready to pursue any reasonable avenue that holds forth the promise of lessening tensions and furthering the prospects of peace. But let our friends and those who may wish us ill take note: the United States has an obligation to its citizens and to the people of the world never to let those who would destroy freedom dictate the future course of life on this planet. I would regard my election as proof that we have renewed our resolve to preserve world peace and freedom. That this nation will once again be strong enough to do that.

Now this evening marks the last step, save one, of a campaign that has taken Nancy and me from one end of this great nation to the other, over many months and thousands and thousands of miles. There are those who question the way we choose a President, who say that our process imposes difficult and exhausting burdens on those who seek the office. I have not found it so.

It is impossible to capture in words the splendor of this vast continent which God has granted as our portion of His creation. There are no words to express the extraordinary strength and character of this breed of people we call Americans. Everywhere we've met thousands of Democrats, Independents and Republicans from all economic conditions, walks of life bound together in that community of shared values of family, work, neighborhood, peace and freedom. They are concerned, yes, they're not frightened. They're disturbed,

stand, now that he's back on shore?

Well, I'll tell you where I stand. I do not favor a peacetime draft or registration, but I do favor pay and benefit levels that will attract and keep highly motivated men and women in our volunteer forces and back them up with an active reserve trained and ready for instant call in case of emergency.

You know, there may be a sailor at the helm of the ship of state, but the ship has no rudder. Critical decisions are made at times almost in comic fashion, but who can laugh?

Who was not embarrassed when the Administration handed a major propaganda victory in the United Nations to the enemies of Israel, our staunch Middle East ally for three decades, and then claimed that the American vote was a "mistake," a "failure of communication" between the President, his Secretary of State and the U.N. Ambassador?

Who does not feel a growing sense of unease as our allies, facing repeated instances of an amateurish and confused Administration, reluctantly conclude that America is unwilling or unable to fulfill its obligations as leader of the free world? Who does not feel rising alarm when the question in any discussion of foreign policy is no longer, "Should we do something?" but "Do we have the capacity to do anything?"

The Administration which has brought us to this state is seeking your endorsement for four more years of weakness, indecision, mediocrity, and incompetence. No. No. No American should vote until he or she has asked: Is the United States stronger and more respected now than it was three-and-a-half years ago? Is the world safer, a safer place in which to live?

It is the responsibility of the President of the United States, in working for peace, to insure that the safety of our people cannot successfully be threatened by a hostile foreign power. As President, fulfilling that responsibility will be my number one priority. We're not a warlike people. Quite the opposite. We always seek to live in peace. We resort to force infrequently and with great reluctance—and only after we've determined that it is absolutely necessary.

arms.

—Our European allies, looking nervously at the growing menace from the East, turn to us for leadership and fail to find it.

—And incredibly, more than 50, as you've been told from this platform so eloquently already, more than 50 of our fellow Americans have been held captive for over eight years—eight months by a dictatorial foreign power that holds us up to ridicule before the world.

Adversaries large and small test our will and seek to confound our resolve, but we are given weakness when we need strength; vacillation when the times demand firmness.

The Carter Administration lives in the world of make-believe. Every day, drawing up a response to that day's problems, troubles, regardless of what happened yesterday and what'll happen tomorrow.

But you and I live in a real world, where disasters are overtaking our nation without any real response from Washington.

This is make-believe, self-deceit and, above all, transparent hypocrisy. For example, Mr. Carter says he supports the volunteer Army, but he lets military pay and benefits slip so low that many of our enlisted personnel are actually eligible for food stamps. Reenlistment rates drop and, just recently, after he fought all week against a proposed pay increase for our men and women in the military, he then helicoptered out to our carrier the U.S.S. *Nimitz*, which was returning from long months of duty in the Indian Ocean, and told the crew of that ship that he advocated better pay for them and their comrades. Where does he really

Metal badge for Reagan convention delegates from Iowa.

A phased reduction of tax rates would go a long way toward easing the heavy burden on the American people. But we shouldn't stop there.

Within the context of economic conditions and appropriate budget priorities during each fiscal year of my Presidency, I would strive to go further. This would include improvement in business depreciation taxes so we can stimulate investment in order to get plants and equipment replaced, put more Americans back to work and put our nation back on the road to being competitive in world commerce. We will also work to reduce the cost of government as a percentage of our gross national product.

The first task of national leadership is to set realistic and honest priorities in our policies and our budget, and I pledge that my administration will do that. When I talk of tax cuts, I am reminded that every major tax cut in this century has strengthened the economy, generated renewed productivity and ended up yielding new revenues for the Government by creating new investment, new jobs and more commerce among our people. [. . .]

It's time to put America back to work, to make our cities and towns resound with the confident voices of men and women of all races, nationalities and faiths bringing home to their families a paycheck they can cash for honest money. For those without skills, we'll find a way to help them get new skills. For those without job opportunities we'll stimulate new opportunities, particularly in the inner cities where they live.

For those who've abandoned hope, we'll restore hope and we'll welcome them into a great national crusade to make America great again.

When we move from domestic affairs, and cast our eyes abroad, we see an equally sorry chapter in the record of the present Administration:

—A Soviet combat brigade trains in Cuba, just 90 miles from our shores.

—A Soviet army of invasion occupies Afghanistan, further threatening our vital interests in the Middle East.

—America's defense strength is at its lowest ebb in a generation, while the Soviet Union is vastly outspending us in both strategic and conventional

tion or Congress. We are going to put an end to the notion that the American taxpayer exists to fund the Federal Government. The Federal Government exists to serve the American people and to be accountable to the American people. On January 20, we are going to reestablish that truth.

Also on that date we are going to initiate action to get substantial relief for our taxpaying citizens and action to put people back to work. None of this will be based on any new form of monetary tinkering or fiscal sleight-of-hand. We will simply apply to government the common sense that we all use in our daily lives.

Work and family are at the center of our lives, the foundation of our dignity as a free people. When we deprive people of what they have earned, or take away their jobs, we destroy their dignity and undermine their families. We can't support families unless there are jobs; and we can't have jobs unless the people have both money to invest and the faith to invest it.

These are concepts that stem from an economic system that for more than 200 years has helped us master a continent, create a previously undreamed-of prosperity for our people and has fed millions of others around the globe and that system will continue to serve us in the future if our Government will stop ignoring the basic values on which it was built and stop betraying the trust and good will of the American workers who keep it going.

The American people are carrying the heaviest peacetime tax burden in our nation's history—and it will grow even heavier, under present law, next January. We are taxing ourselves into economic exhaustion and stagnation, crushing our ability and incentive to save, invest and produce.

This must stop. We must halt this fiscal self-destruction and restore sanity to our economic system.

I've long advocated a 30 percent reduction in income tax rates over a period of three years. This phased tax reduction would begin with a 10 percent "down payment" tax cut in 1981, which the Republicans in Congress and I have already proposed.

ment. Our problems are both acute and chronic, yet all we hear from those in positions of leadership are the same tired proposals for more Government tinkering, more meddling and more control—all of which led us to this sorry state in the first place. Can anyone look at the record of this Administration and say, "Well done"?

Can anyone compare the state of our economy when the Carter Administration took office with where we are today and say, "Keep up the good work"? Can anyone look at our reduced standing in the world today and say, "Let's have four more years of this"?

I believe the American people are going to answer these questions, as you've answered them, in the first week of November and their answer will be, "No—we've had enough." And then it will be up to us—beginning next January 20—to offer an Administration and Congressional leadership of competence and more than a little courage.

We must have the clarity of vision to see the difference between what is essential and what is merely desirable; and then the courage to bring our Government back under control.

It is essential that we maintain both the forward momentum of economic growth and the strength of the safety net between those in our society who need help. We also believe it is essential that the integrity of all aspects of Social Security be preserved.

Beyond these essentials, I believe it is clear our Federal Government is overgrown and overweight. Indeed, it is time our Government should go on a diet. Therefore, my first act as chief executive will be to impose an immediate and thorough freeze on Federal hiring. Then, we are going to enlist the very best minds from business, labor and whatever quarter to conduct a detailed review of every department, bureau and agency that lives by Federal appropriation. [. . .]

I will not accept the excuse that the Federal Government has grown so big and powerful that it is beyond the control of any President, any administra-

First, we must overcome something the present Administration has cooked up: a new and altogether indigestible economic stew, one part inflation, one part high unemployment, one part recession, one part runaway taxes, one part deficit spending seasoned with an energy crisis. It's an economic stew that has turned the national stomach.

Ours are not problems of abstract economic theory. These are problems of flesh and blood; problems that cause pain and destroy the moral fiber of real people who should not suffer the further indignity of being told by the Government that it is all somehow their fault. We do not have inflation because—as Mr. Carter says—we've lived too well.

The head of a Government which has utterly refused to live within its means and which has, in the last few days, told us that this coming year's deficit will be $60 billion, dares to point the finger of blame at business and labor, both of which have been engaged in a losing struggle just trying to stay even.

High taxes, we are told, are somehow good for us, as if, when government spends our money it isn't inflationary, but when we spend it, it is.

Those who preside over the worst energy shortage in our history tell us to use less so that we will run out of oil, gasoline and natural gas a little more slowly. Well, now, conservation is desirable, of course, but we must not waste energy. But conservation is not the sole answer to our energy needs.

America must get to work producing more energy. The Republican program for solving economic problems is based on growth and productivity.

Large amounts of oil and natural gas lay beneath our land and off our shores, untouched because the present Administration seems to believe the American people would rather see more regulation, more taxes and more controls than more energy. [. . .]

Now make no mistake. We will not permit the safety of our people or our environmental heritage to be jeopardized, but we are going to reaffirm that the economic prosperity of our people is a fundamental part of our environ-

Celluloid button for Bush distributed at the 1980 Republican convention.

George H. Bush had held a series of prestigious posts—among them U. S. ambassador to the United Nations, envoy to China, and director of the Central Intelligence Agency. On the strength of his impressive resume, Bush decided to run for president in 1980. He presented himself as a moderate Republican who favored some government activism to address social problems. Despite philosophical differences and Bush's harsh words about Reagan's economic ideas, Reagan picked Bush to be his running mate in an attempt to present a more ideologically balanced ticket.

Let us pledge to restore, in our time, the American spirit of voluntary service, of cooperation, of private and community initiative; a spirit that flows like a deep and mighty river through the history of our nation.

As your nominee, I pledge to you to restore to the Federal Government the capacity to do the people's work without dominating their lives. I pledge to you a Government that will not only work well but wisely, its ability to act tempered by prudence, and its willingness to do good balanced by the knowledge that government is never more dangerous than when our desire to have it help us blinds us to its great power to harm us.

You know, the first Republican President once said, "While the people retain their virtue and their vigilance, no Administration by any extreme of wickedness or folly can seriously injure the Government in the short space of four years." If Mr. Lincoln could see what's happened in these last three and a half years, he might hedge a little on that statement. But with the virtues that are our legacy as a free people and with the vigilance that sustains liberty, we still have time to use our renewed compact to overcome the injuries that have been done to America these past three and a half years.

others by moving backward ourselves. And those who believe we can have no business leading this nation.

I will not stand by and watch this great country destroy itself under mediocre leadership that drifts from one crisis to the next, eroding our national will and purpose. We have come together here because the American people deserve better from those to whom they entrust our nation's highest offices, and we stand united in our resolve to do something about it.

We need a rebirth of the American tradition of leadership at every level of government and in private life as well. The United States of America is unique in world history because it has a genius for leaders—many leaders—on many levels. But back in 1976, Mr. Carter said, "Trust me." And a lot of people did. And now, many of those people are out of work. Many have seen their savings eaten away by inflation. Many others on fixed incomes, especially the elderly, have watched helplessly as the cruel tax of inflation wasted away their purchasing power. And, today, a great many who trusted Mr. Carter wonder if we can survive the Carter policies of national defense.

"Trust me" government asks that we concentrate our hopes and dreams on one man; that we trust him to do what's best for us. But my view of government places trust not in one person or one party, but in those values that transcend persons and parties. The trust is where it belongs—in the people. The responsibility to live up to that trust is where it belongs, in their elected leaders. That kind of relationship, between the people and their elected leaders, is a special kind of compact. [. . .]

Isn't it once again time to renew our compact of freedom; to pledge to each other all that is best in our lives; all that gives meaning to them—for the sake of this, our beloved and blessed land?

Together, let us make this a new beginning. Let us make a commitment to care for the needy; to teach our children the values handed down to us by our families; to have the courage to defend those values and virtues and the willingness to sacrifice for them.

With a deep awareness of the responsibility conferred by your trust, I accept your nomination for the Presidency of the United States. I do so with deep gratitude. And I think also I might interject on behalf of all of us our thanks to Detroit and the people of Michigan and to this city for the warm hospitality we've enjoyed. And I thank you for your whole-hearted response to my recommendation in regard to George Bush as the candidate for Vice President.

I'm very proud of our party tonight. This convention has shown to all America a party united, with positive programs for solving the nation's problems, a party ready to build a new consensus with all those across the land who share a community of values embodied in these words: family, work, neighborhood, peace and freedom.

Now I know we've had a quarrel or two but only as to the method of attaining a goal. There was no argument here about the goal. [. . .]

Never before in our history have Americans been called upon to face three grave threats to our very existence, any one of which could destroy us. We face a disintegrating economy, a weakened defense and an energy policy based on the sharing of scarcity.

The major issue in this campaign is the direct political, personal, and moral responsibility of Democratic Party leadership—in the White House and in the Congress—for this unprecedented calamity which has befallen us. They tell us they've done the most that humanly could be done. They say that the United States has had its day in the sun, that our nation has passed its zenith. They expect you to tell your children that the American people no longer have the will to cope with their problems; that the future will be one of sacrifice and few opportunities.

My fellow citizens, I utterly reject that view. The American people, the most generous on earth, who created the highest standard of living, are not going to accept the notion that we can only make a better world for

but not dismayed. They are the kind of men and women Tom Paine had in mind when he wrote, during the darkest days of the American Revolution, "We have it in our power to begin the world over again." [. . .]

The time is now to resolve that the basis of a firm and principled foreign policy is one that takes the world as it is and seeks to change it by leadership and example, not by harangue, harassment or wishful thinking.

The time is now to say that we shall seek new friendships and expand others and improve others, but we shall not do so by breaking our word or casting aside old friends and allies. [. . .]

The time is now, my fellow Americans, to recapture our destiny, to take it into our own hands. And to do this it will take many of us, working together. I ask you tonight, all over this land, to volunteer your help in this cause so that we can carry our message through out the land.

Isn't it time that we, the people, carry out these unkept promises? That we pledge to each other and to all America [. . .] that now we intend to do just that.

I have thought of something that's not a part of my speech and worried over whether I should do it. Can we doubt that only a Divine Providence placed this land, this island of freedom, here as a refuge for all those people in the world who yearn to breathe free? Jews and Christians enduring persecution behind the Iron Curtain; the boat people of Southeast Asia, Cuba, and of Haiti; the victims of drought and famine in Africa, the freedom fighters of Afghanistan, and our own countrymen held in savage captivity.

I'll confess that I've been a little afraid to suggest what I'm going to suggest. I'm more afraid not to. Can we begin our crusade joined together in a moment of silent prayer?

God bless America.

Thank you.

said that there are times in our history when concerns over our personal lives are overshadowed by concern for "what will happen to the country we have known." This is such a time—and I can tell you that the choice to be made this year can transform our own personal lives and the life of our country as well.

During the last presidential campaign, I crisscrossed this country and I listened to thousands and thousands of people—housewives and farmers, teachers and small-business leaders, workers and students, the elderly and the poor—people of every race and every background and every walk of life. It was a powerful experience—a total immersion in the human reality of America.

And I have now had another kind of total immersion—being president of the United States of America. Let me talk for a moment about what that job is like—and what I have learned from it.

I've learned that only the most complex and difficult tasks come before me in the Oval Office. No easy answers are found there—because no easy questions come there.

I've learned that for a president, experience is the best guide to the right decisions. I'm wiser tonight than I was four years ago.

And I have learned that the presidency is a place of compassion. My own heart is burdened for the troubled Americans. The poor and the jobless and the afflicted—they've become part of me. My thoughts and my prayers for our hostages in Iran are as though they were my own sons and daughters. [. . .]

The president is a servant of today. But his true constituency is the future. That is why the election of 1980 is so important.

Some have said it makes no difference who wins this election. They are wrong. This election is a stark choice between two men, two parties, two sharply different pictures of what America is and what the world is. But it is more than that.

It is a choice between two futures. The year 2000 is just less than 20 years away—just four presidential elections after this one. Children born this year

Celluloid button sold by New York City vendors during the Democratic national convention.

will come of age in the 21st century.

The time to shape the world of the year 2000 is now. The decisions of the next few years will set our course, per-haps an irreversible course—and the most important of all choices will be made by the American people at the polls less than three months from tonight.

The choice could not be more clear—nor the consequences more crucial.

In one of the futures we can choose—the future that you and I have been building together—I see security and justice and peace.

I see a future of security that will come from tapping our own great resources of oil and gas, coal and sunlight—and from building the tools, the technology and factories for a revitalized economy based on jobs and stable prices for everyone.

I see a future of justice—the justice of good jobs, decent health care, quality education, and the full opportunity for all people, regardless of color or language or religion; the simple human justice of equal rights for all men—and for all women, guaranteed equal rights at last—under the Constitution of the United States of America.

And I see a future of peace—a peace born of wisdom and based on the fair-ness toward all countries of the world—a peace guaranteed both by American military strength and by American moral strength as well.

That is the future I want for all people—a future of confidence and hope and a good life. It is the future America must choose—and with your help and with your commitment, it is the future America will choose.

1980 campaign items. Television commercials and sound bites effectively conveyed the candidates' message. Carter ephemera often portrayed him as a solemn world statesman.

But there is another possible future.

In that other future, I see despair—the despair of millions who would struggle for equal opportunity and a better life—and struggle alone.

And I see surrender—the surrender of our energy future to the merchants of oil, the surrender of our economic future to a bizarre program of massive tax cuts for the rich, service cuts for the poor and massive inflation for everyone.

And I see risk—the risk of international confrontation: the risk of an uncontrollable, unaffordable, and unwinnable nuclear arms race.

No one, Democrat or Republican leader, consciously seeks such a future. And I do not claim that my opponent does. But I do question the disturbing commitments and policies already made by him and by those with him who have now captured control of the Republican Party.

The consequences of those commitments and policies would drive us down the wrong road. It's up to all of us to make sure America rejects this alarming, and even perilous, destiny. [. . .]

You and I have been working toward a secure future by rebuilding our military strength—steadily, carefully and responsibly. The Republicans talk about military strength—but they were in office for eight out of the last 11 years, and in the face of a growing Soviet threat they steadily cut real defense spending by more than a third.

We've reversed the Republican decline in defense. Every year since I've been president, we've had real increases in our commitment to a stronger nation—increases which are prudent and rational. There is no doubt that the United States of America can meet any threat from the Soviet Union. [. . .]

The new leaders of the Republican Party, in order to close the gap between their rhetoric and their record, have now promised to launch an all-out nuclear arms race. This would negate any further effort to negotiate a strategic arms limitation agreement.

There can be no winners in such an arms race—and all the people of the Earth can be the losers.

The Republican nominee advocates abandoning arms control policies which have been important and supported by every Democratic president since Harry Truman and also by every Republican president since Dwight D. Eisenhower. This radical and irresponsible course would threaten our security—and could put the whole world in peril.

You and I must never let this come to pass.

It's simple to call for a new arms race. But when armed aggression threatens world peace, tough-sounding talk like that is not enough. A president must act—responsibly. When Soviet troops invaded Afghanistan, we moved quickly to take action. I suspended some grain sales to the Soviet Union. I called for draft registration. We joined wholeheartedly with the Congress. And I joined wholeheartedly with the Congress and with the U.S. Olympic Committee and led more than 60 other nations in boycotting the big propaganda show in Russia—the Moscow Olympics.

The Republican leader opposed two of these forceful but peaceful actions and he waffled on the third. But when we asked him what he would do about aggression in Southwest Asia, he suggested blockading Cuba. Even his running mate wouldn't go along with that.

He doesn't seem to know what to do with the Russians. He's not sure if he wants to feed them or play with them or fight with them.

As I look back on my first term, I'm grateful that we've had a country with a full four years of peace. And that's what we're going to have for the next four years—peace. [. . .] Before I became president there was no Camp David accord and there was no Middle East peace treaty. Before Camp David, Israel and Egypt were poised across barbed wire, confronting each other with guns and tanks and planes. But afterward, they talked face-to-face with each other across a peace table—and they also communicated through their own ambassadors in Cairo and Tel Aviv.

Now that's the kind of future we're offering—of peace in the Middle East if the Democrats are reelected in the fall. [. . .]

When I took office, I inherited a heavy load of serious economic problems besides energy—and we've met them all head-on. We've slashed government regulation and put free enterprise back into the airlines, the trucking and the financial systems of our country—and we're now doing the same thing for the railroads. This is the greatest change in the relationship between government and business since the New Deal.

We've increased our exports dramatically. We've reversed the decline in the basic research and development. And we have created more than 8 million new jobs—the biggest increase in the history of our country. [. . .]

We are now at a critical turning point in our economic history. [. . .] Our economic renewal program for the 1980s will meet our immediate need for jobs by attacking the very same long-term problems that caused unemployment and inflation in the first place. It will move America simultaneously towards our five great economic goals—lower inflation, better productivity, revitalization of American industry, energy security, and jobs. [. . .]

The Republican alternative is the biggest tax giveaway in history. They call it "Reagan-Kemp-Roth." I call it a free lunch America can not afford. [. . .]

Now I don't claim perfection for the Democratic Party. I don't claim that every decision that we have made has been right or popular. Certainly they've not all been easy. But I will say this: We've been tested under fire. We've neither ducked nor hidden. And we've tackled the great, central issues of our time, the historic challenges of peace and energy which had been ignored for years.

We've made tough decisions and we've taken the heat for them. We've made mistakes and we've learned from them. So we have built the foundation now for a better future. [. . .]

The choice—the choice between the two futures—could not be more clear. If we succumb to a dream world, then we'll wake up in a nightmare. But if we start with reality and fight to make our dreams a reality—then Americans will have a good life, a life of meaning and purpose in a nation that's strong and secure.

Above all, I want us to be what the founders of our nation meant us to become—the land of freedom, the land of peace, and the land of hope.

Thank you very much.

First Inaugural Address

The 1981 inauguration was held for the first time on the west side of the Capitol. Ronald Reagan took the oath of office with his hand on his mother's Bible opened to the seventh chapter, fourteenth verse of Second Chronicles, "If my people . . . shall humble themselves and pray . . . and turn from their wicked ways, then will I . . . forgive their sin, and will heal their land." Next to these words, his mother had written, "A most wonderful verse for the healing of nations."

Carter, in the last days of his presidency, had concluded months of negotiations by agreeing to release several billion dollars in Iranian assets that he had frozen in American banks shortly after the seizure of the embassy. As Reagan was being sworn in, the American hostages, after their 444-day ordeal, were released.

To a few of us here today, this is a solemn and most momentous occasion; and yet, in the history of our Nation, it is a commonplace occurrence. The orderly transfer of authority as called for in the Constitution routinely takes place as it has for almost two centuries and few of us stop to think how unique we really are. In the eyes of many in the world, this every-four-year ceremony we accept as normal is nothing less than a miracle.

Mr. President, I want our fellow citizens to know how much you did to carry on this tradition. By your gracious cooperation in the transition process, you have shown a watching world that we are a united people pledged to maintaining a political system which guarantees individual liberty to a greater degree than any other, and I thank you and your people for all your help in maintaining the continuity which is the bulwark of our Republic.

The business of our nation goes forward. These United States are confronted with an economic affliction of great proportions. We suffer from the longest and one of the worst sustained inflations in our national history. It distorts our economic decisions, penalizes thrift, and crushes the struggling young and the fixed-income elderly alike. It threatens to shatter the lives of millions of our people.

Idle industries have cast workers into unemployment, causing human misery and personal indignity. Those who do work are denied a fair return for their labor by a tax system which penalizes successful achievement and keeps us from maintaining full productivity.

But great as our tax burden is, it has not kept pace with public spending. For decades, we have piled deficit upon deficit, mortgaging our future and our children's future for the temporary convenience of the present. To continue this long trend is to guarantee tremendous social, cultural, political, and economic upheavals.

You and I, as individuals, can, by borrowing, live beyond our means,

★ National Address ★ on the Economy

Reagan made a strong first impression as president. He focused on recovery from what he called "the worst economic mess since the Great Depression." He proposed increased military spending, reduced income-tax rates, and cutbacks in various domestic programs. Reagan's agenda was widely hailed by conservatives and denounced by liberals.

Reagan, often called the Great Communicator, had the ability to mobilize public opinion. During this address on the economy, the president explained the nation's difficulties by holding a dollar in one hand and 36 cents in the other to show how inflation had eroded the dollar's value over the previous 20 years. He asked support for his plan to turn the economy around. Reagan's speech resulted in an unusually large number of letters, calls, and telegrams. By late 1981, Congress had enacted into law most of his program.

I'm speaking to you tonight to give you a report on the state of our Nation's economy. I regret to say that we're in the worst economic mess since the Great Depression.

A few days ago I was presented with a report I'd asked for, a comprehensive audit, if you will, of our economic condition. You won't like it. I didn't like it. But we have to face the truth and then go to work to turn things around. And make no mistake about it, we can turn them around.

I'm not going to subject you to the jumble of charts, figures, and economic jargon of that audit, but rather will try to explain where we are, how we got there, and how we can get back. First, however, let me just give a few "attention getters" from the audit.

The Federal budget is out of control, and we face runaway deficits of almost $80 billion for this budget year that ends September 30th. That deficit is larger than the entire Federal budget in 1957, and so is the almost $80 billion we will pay in interest this year on the national debt.

Twenty years ago, in 1960, our Federal Government payroll was less than $13 billion. Today it is $75 billion. During these 20 years our population has only increased by 23.3 percent. The Federal budget has gone up 528 percent.

Now, we've just had two years of back-to-back double-digit inflation—13.3 percent in 1979, 12.4 percent last year. The last time this happened was in World War I.

In 1960 mortgage interest rates averaged about 6 percent. They're two-and-a-half times as high now, 15.4 percent.

The percentage of your earnings the Federal Government took in taxes in 1960 has almost doubled.

And finally there are 7 million Americans caught up in the personal indignity and human tragedy of unemployment. If they stood in a line, allowing 3 feet for each person, the line would reach from the coast of

Maine to California.

Well, so much for the audit itself. Let me try to put this in personal terms. Here is a dollar such as you earned, spent, or saved in 1960. And here is a quarter, a dime, and a penny—36 cents. That's what this 1960 dollar is worth today. And if the present world inflation rate should continue 3 more years, that dollar of 1960 will be worth a quarter. What initiative is there to save? And if we don't save we're short of the investment capital needed for business and industry expansion. Workers in Japan and West Germany save several times the percentage of their income than Americans do.

What's happened to that American dream of owning a home? Only 10 years ago a family could buy a home, and the monthly payment averaged little more than a quarter—27 cents out of each dollar earned. Today, it takes 42 cents out of every dollar of income. So, fewer than 1 out of 11 families can afford to buy their first new home.

Regulations adopted by government with the best of intentions have added $666 to the cost of an automobile. It is estimated that altogether regulations of every kind, on shopkeepers, farmers, and major industries, add $100 billion or more to the cost of the goods and services we buy. And then another $20 billion is spent by government handling the paperwork created by those regulations.

I'm sure you're getting the idea that the audit presented to me found government policies of the last few decades responsible for our economic troubles. We forgot or just overlooked the fact that government—any government—has a built-in tendency to grow. Now, we all had a hand in looking to government for benefits as if government had some source of revenue other than our earnings. Many if not most of the things we thought of or that government offered to us seemed attractive.

In the years following the Second World War it was easy, for a while at least, to overlook the price tag. Our income more than doubled in the 25 years after the war. We increased our take-home pay in those 25 years by more than we had amassed in all the preceding 150 years put together. Yes, there was some inflation, 1 or 1-1/2 percent a year. That didn't bother us. But if we look back at those golden years, we recall that even then voices had been raised, warning that inflation, like radioactivity, was cumulative and that once started it could get out of control.

Some government programs seemed so worthwhile that borrowing to fund them didn't bother us. By 1960 our national debt stood at $284 billion. Congress in 1971 decided to put a ceiling of $400 billion on our ability to borrow. Today the debt is $934 billion. So-called temporary increases or extensions in the debt ceiling have been allowed 21 times in these 10 years, and now I've been forced to ask for another increase in the debt ceiling or the government will be unable to function past the middle of February—and I've only been here 16 days. Before we reach the day when we can reduce the debt ceiling, we may in spite of our best efforts see a national debt in excess of a trillion dollars. Now, this is a figure that's literally beyond our comprehension.

We know now that inflation results from all that deficit spending. Government has only two ways of getting money other than raising taxes. It can go into the money market and borrow, competing with its own citizens and driving up interest rates, which it has done, or it can print money, and it's done that. Both methods are inflationary.

We're victims of language. The very word "inflation" leads us to think of it as just high prices. Then, of course, we resent the person who puts on the price tags, forgetting that he or she is also a victim of inflation. Inflation is not just high prices; it's a reduction in the value of our money. When the money supply is increased but the goods and services available for buying are not, we have too much money chasing too few goods. Wars are usually accompanied by inflation. Everyone is working or fighting, but production is of weapons and munitions, not things we can buy and use.

Now, one way out would be to raise taxes so that government need not borrow or print money. But in all these years of government growth, we've reached, indeed surpassed, the limit of our people's tolerance or ability to bear an increase in the tax burden. Prior to World War II, taxes were such that on the average we only had to work just a little over 1 month each year to pay our total Federal, State, and local tax bill. Today we have to work 4 months to pay that bill.

Some say shift the tax burden to business and industry, but business doesn't pay taxes. Oh, don't get the wrong idea. Business is being taxed, so much so that we're being priced out of the world market. But business must pass its costs of operations—and that includes taxes—on to the customer in the price of the product. Only people pay taxes, all the taxes. Government just uses business in a kind of sneaky way to help collect the taxes. They're hidden in the price; we aren't aware of how much tax we actually pay.

Today this once great industrial giant of ours has the lowest rate of gain in productivity of virtually all the industrial nations with whom we must compete in the world market. We can't even hold our own market here in America against foreign automobiles, steel, and a number of other products. Japanese production of automobiles is almost twice as great per worker as it is in America. Japanese steelworkers outproduce their American counterparts by about 25 percent.

Now, this isn't because they're better workers. I'll match the American working man or woman against anyone in the world. But we have to give them the tools and equipment that workers in the other industrial nations have.

We invented the assembly line and mass production, but punitive tax policies and excessive and unnecessary regulations plus government borrowing have stifled our ability to update plant and equipment. When capital investment is made, it's too often for some unproductive alterations demanded by government to meet various of its regulations. Excessive taxation of individuals has robbed us of incentive and made overtime unprofitable.

We once produced about 40 percent of the world's steel. We now produce 19 percent. We were once the greatest producer of automobiles, producing more

Two-sided cloth doll satirizing Reaganomics. Reaganomics—or supply-side economics—is a series of economic policies enacted into laws which were espoused and implemented by Ronald Reagan during his presidency.

than all the rest of the world combined. That is no longer true, and in addition, the "Big Three," the major auto companies in our land, have sustained tremendous losses in the past year and have been forced to lay off thousands of workers.

All of you who are working know that even with cost-of-living pay raises, you can't keep up with inflation. In our progressive tax system, as you increase the number of dollars you earn, you find yourself moved up into higher tax brackets, paying a higher tax rate just for trying to hold your own. The result? Your standard of living is going down.

Over the past decades we've talked of curtailing government spending so that we can then lower the tax burden. Sometimes we've even taken a run at doing that. But there were always those who told us that taxes couldn't be cut until spending was reduced. Well, you know, we can lecture our children about extravagance until we run out of voice and breath. Or we can cure their extravagance by simply reducing their allowance.

It's time to recognize that we've come to a turning point. We're threatened with an economic calamity of tremendous proportions, and the old business-

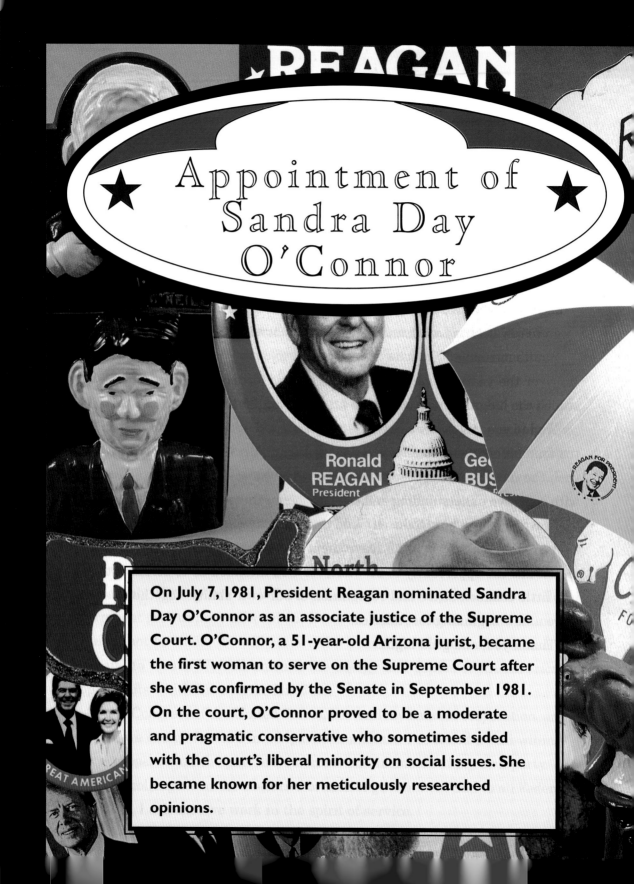

Appointment of Sandra Day O'Connor

On July 7, 1981, President Reagan nominated Sandra Day O'Connor as an associate justice of the Supreme Court. O'Connor, a 51-year-old Arizona jurist, became the first woman to serve on the Supreme Court after she was confirmed by the Senate in September 1981. On the court, O'Connor proved to be a moderate and pragmatic conservative who sometimes sided with the court's liberal minority on social issues. She became known for her meticulously researched opinions.

As President of the United States, I have the honor and the privilege to pick thousands of appointees for positions in Federal Government. Each is important and deserves a great deal of care for each individual called upon make his or her contribution, often at personal sacrifice, to shaping the policy of the Nation. Thus each has an obligation to you, in varying degrees, has an impact on your life.

In addition, as President, I have the privilege to make a certain number of nominations which have a more lasting influence on our lives, for they are the lifetime appointments of those men and women called upon to serve in the judiciary in our Federal district courts and courts of appeals. These individuals dispense justice and provide for us these most cherished guarantees of protections of our criminal and civil laws. But, without doubt, the most awesome appointment is a guarantee to us of so many things, because [. . .] as a President, I can make an appointment to the United States Supreme Court.

Those who sit in the Supreme Court interpret the laws of our land and truly do leave their footprints on the sands of time. Long after the policies of Presidents and Senators and Congressmen of any given era may have passed from public memory, they'll be remembered.

After very careful review and consideration, I have made the decision as to my nominee to fill the vacancy on the United States Supreme Court created by the resignation of Justice Stewart. Since I am aware of the great amount of speculation about this appointment, I want to share this very important decision with you as soon as possible.

Needless to say, most of the speculation has centered on the question of whether I would consider a woman to fill this first vacancy. As the press has accurately pointed out, during my campaign for the Presidency I made a commitment that one of my first appointments to the Supreme Court vacancy would be the most qualified woman that I could possibly find.

White House press release

Nomination of Sandra Day O'Connor to be an Associate Justice of the Supreme Court of the United States

July 7, 1981—The President today announced his intention to nominate Judge Sandra Day O'Connor to be an Associate Justice of the Supreme Court of the United States, filling the vacancy created by the resignation of Justice Potter Stewart. Judge O'Connor presently serves on the Arizona Court of Appeals. The President will forward to the Senate his nomination of Judge O'Connor upon completion of the required background check by the Federal Bureau of Investigation.

Judge O'Connor, age 51, earned both her undergraduate and law degrees at Stanford University. She received her B.A. magna cum laude in 1950 and her LL.B. with high honors in 1952. She was a member of the board of editors of the Stanford Law Review and a member of the Order of the Coif. Judge O'Connor was admitted to the Bar of the State of California in the year of her graduation and to the Bar of the State of Arizona in 1957.

Judge O'Connor practiced law in Phoenix, Ariz., for a number of years. She served as assistant attorney general of Arizona from 1965 to 1969 and served in the Arizona State Senate from 1969 to 1975.

In 1974 Judge O'Connor was elected to the superior court for Maricopa County, Ariz. She served on that court until she was appointed to the Arizona Court of Appeals in 1979.

Judge O'Connor is married to John Hay O'Connor III. They have three children.

Now, this is not to say that I would appoint a woman merely to do so. That would not be fair to women nor to future generations of all Americans whose lives are so deeply affected by decisions of the Court. Rather, I pledged to appoint a woman who meets the very high standards that I demand of all court appointees. I have identified such a person.

So today, I'm pleased to announce that upon completion of all the necessary checks by the Federal Bureau of Investigation, I will send to the Senate the nomination of Judge Sandra Day O'Connor of Arizona Court of Appeals for confirmation as an Associate Justice of the United States Supreme Court.

She is truly a person for all seasons, possessing those unique qualities of temperament, fairness, intellectual capacity, and devotion to the public good which have characterized the 101 brethren who have preceded her. I commend her to you, and I urge the Senate's swift bipartisan confirmation so that as soon as possible she may take her seat on the Court and her place in history.

> **During the 1980s, a significant change occurred in the workforce. The number of working women almost doubled in the twenty years between 1960 and 1980. Increasingly, women were holding jobs at all levels. Between 1970 and 1980 the number of women in management positions grew by about 50 percent. More women were becoming professionals. The number of women lawyers tripled between 1970 and 1980, and women physicians rose in number by 50 percent. Women moved into fields that had long been closed to them—the construction trades, police and fire departments, among many others. However, two symbolic breakthroughs occurred when President Reagan appointed Sandra Day O'Connor as the first woman justice of the Supreme Court in 1981 and when astronaut Sally Ride orbited aboard the space shuttle in 1983 as the first American woman in space.**

The Air Traffic Controllers Strike

Ronald
REAGAN
President

Ge
BUS

REAGAN FOR PRESIDENT

North
Dakota
—

REAGAN COUNTRY

At 10:55 A.M. August 3, 1981, President Reagan spoke with reporters in the White House Rose Garden. The members of the air traffic controllers union (PATCO) had agreed to strike earlier that morning, in defiance of a federal order. Reagan gave the strikers 48 hours to return to the job, and fired those who did not.

This morning at 7 A.M. the union representing those who man America's air traffic control facilities called a strike. This was the culmination of seven months of negotiations between the Federal Aviation Administration and the union. At one point in these negotiations agreement was reached and signed by both sides, granting a $40 million increase in salaries and benefits. This is twice what other government employees can expect. It was granted in recognition of the difficulties inherent in the work these people perform. Now, however, the union demands are 17 times what had been agreed to—$681 million. This would impose a tax burden on their fellow citizens which is unacceptable.

I would like to thank the supervisors and controllers who are on the job today, helping to get the nation's air system operating safely. In the New York area, for example, four supervisors were scheduled to report for work, and 17 additionally volunteered. At National Airport a traffic controller told a newsperson he had resigned from the union and reported to work because, "How can I ask my kids to obey the law if I don't?" This is a great tribute to America.

Let me make one thing plain. I respect the right of workers in the private sector to strike. Indeed, as president of my own union, I led the first strike ever called by that union. I guess I'm maybe the first one to ever hold this office who is a lifetime member of an AFL-CIO union. But we cannot compare labor-management relations in the private sector with government. Government cannot close down the assembly line. It has to provide without interruption the protective services which are government's reason for being.

It was in recognition of this that the Congress passed a law forbidding strikes by government employees against the public safety. Let me read the solemn oath taken by each of these employees, a sworn affidavit, when they accepted their jobs: "I am not participating in any strike against the

Two defining events occurred early in the Reagan presidency. One was an attempt on Reagan's life on March 30, 1981. A deranged John W. Hinkley Jr. shot and wounded Reagan and his press secretary before he was overcome. The bullet that struck Reagan lodged within an inch of his heart, narrowly missing the vital aorta by about the same distance. Reagan was rushed to a Washington hospital where he won the admiration of the American people for a seemingly carefree remark on the operating

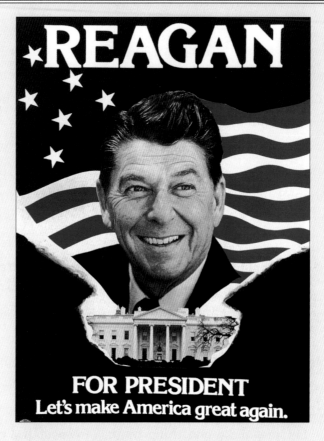

REAGAN

FOR PRESIDENT
Let's make America great again.

table: "Please tell me you're Republicans," he quipped to the doctors who were preparing him for surgery.

The other defining moment of Reagan's first year in office took place on August 3, 1981. Ignoring a law that forbade them to strike, the nation's air traffic controllers walked off their jobs to press their demands. (The union had been one of the few to endorse Reagan in the 1980 election.) Reagan ordered the controllers back to work, but they refused, thinking the airlines could not function without them. The president responded by firing more than 1,100 controllers and establishing programs to train replacements. When the strike collapsed, the president refused to rehire any of the strikers. Reagan said later that his action "convinced people who might have thought otherwise that I meant what I said."

(Opposite) This poster for Reagan, issued by the Republican National Committee during the 1980 campaign, included Reagan's favorite slogan. (Right) Movie lobby card. In addition to being a film actor, Ronald Reagan was the first president to be a union member as well as the head of a union, the Screen Actors Guild (1947–52; 1959).

Government of the United States or any agency thereof, and I will not so participate while an employee of the Government of the United States or any agency thereof."

It is for this reason that I must tell those who fail to report for duty this morning they are in violation of the law, and if they do not report for work within 48 hours, they have forfeited their jobs and will be terminated.

"Evil Empire" Speech

President Reagan entered office in a world largely controlled by two superpowers—the United States and the Soviet Union—each with vast resources, far-flung alliances of client states, and ever-costlier arms systems constantly stimulated by technological innovations. For 25 years prior to his 1980 election, Reagan had delivered thousands of speeches to friendly conservative audiences who shared his assurances that world affairs simply reflected the biblical struggle between the forces of good and evil. Reagan's supporters have insisted that his seemingly simplistic worldview actually masked his political genius—which he chose to communicate in stark terms to be better understood. As president, Reagan dealt with the Soviet Union both with bellicose rhetoric and traditional diplomacy. He attended four summit conferences with the Soviet leadership. Reagan also offered this assessment of the Soviet Union as an "evil empire" at a conference of Evangelicals in 1983.

There is sin and evil in the world, and we're enjoined by Scripture and the Lord Jesus to oppose it with all our might. Our nation, too, has a legacy of evil with which it must deal. The glory of this land has been its capacity for transcending the moral evils of our past. For example, the long struggle of our minority citizens for equal rights, once a source of disunity and civil war, is now a source of pride for all Americans. We must never go back. There is no room for racism, anti-Semitism, or other forms of ethnic and racial hatred in this country.

I know that you've been horrified, as have I, by the resurgence of some hate groups preaching bigotry and prejudice. Use the mighty voice of your pulpits and the powerful standing of your churches to denounce and isolate these hate groups in our midst. The commandment given us is clear and simple: "Thou shalt love thy neighbor as thyself."

But whatever sad episodes exist in our past, any objective observer must hold a positive view of American history, a history that has been the story of hopes fulfilled and dreams made into reality. Especially in this century, America has kept alight the torch of freedom, but not just for ourselves but for millions of others around the world.

And this brings me to my final point today. During my first press conference as President, in answer to a direct question, I pointed out that, as good Marxist-Leninists, the Soviet leaders have openly and publicly declared that the only morality they recognize is that which will further their cause, which is world revolution. I think I should point out that I was only quoting Lenin, their guiding spirit, who said in 1920 that they repudiate all morality that proceeds from supernatural ideas—that's their name for religion—or ideas that are outside class conceptions. Morality is entirely subordinate to the interests of class war. And everything is moral that is necessary for the annihilation of the old, exploiting social order and for uniting the proletariat.

The "Star Wars" Missile Defense Concept

Ronald
REAGAN
President

Ge
BUS

Early Reagan Administration foreign policy encouraged the futuristic concept of the Strategic Defense Initiative, popularly known as "Star Wars," after the then-current science fiction film. This plan promised to secure the United States against incoming missiles with an extraterrestrial shield. "Perfect security," as claimed by its supporters, would, in effect, end the threat of nuclear war. While his administration resumed arms control talks with the Soviet Union, Reagan remained committed to the Star Wars concept throughout his term.

My fellow Americans, thank you for sharing your time with me tonight.

The subject I want to discuss with you, peace and national security, is both timely and important. Timely, because I've reached a decision which offers a new hope for our children in the 21st century, a decision I'll tell you about in a few minutes. And important because there's a very big decision that you must make for yourselves. This subject involves the most basic duty that any President and any people share, the duty to protect and strengthen the peace. [. . .]

There was a time when we depended on coastal forts and artillery batteries, because, with the weaponry of that day, any attack would have had to come by sea. Well, this is a different world, and our defenses must be based on recognition and awareness of the weaponry possessed by other nations in the nuclear age.

We can't afford to believe that we will never be threatened. There have been two world wars in my lifetime. We didn't start them and, indeed, did everything we could to avoid being drawn into them. But we were ill-prepared for both. Had we been better prepared, peace might have been preserved.

For 20 years the Soviet Union has been accumulating enormous military might. They didn't stop when their forces exceeded all requirements of a legitimate defensive capability. And they haven't stopped now. During the past decade and a half, the Soviets have built up a massive arsenal of new strategic nuclear weapons—weapons that can strike directly at the United States. [. . .]

When I took office in January 1981, I was appalled by what I found: American planes that couldn't fly and American ships that couldn't sail for lack of spare parts and trained personnel and insufficient fuel and ammunition for essential training. The inevitable result of all this was poor morale in our Armed Forces, difficulty in recruiting the brightest young Americans to wear the uniform, and difficulty in convincing our most experienced military personnel to stay on.

There was a real question then about how well we could meet a crisis. And it was obvious that we had to begin a major modernization program to ensure we could deter aggression and preserve the peace in the years ahead. [. . .]

If the Soviet Union will join with us in our effort to achieve major arms reduction, we will have succeeded in stabilizing the nuclear balance. Nevertheless, it will still be necessary to rely on the specter of retaliation, on mutual threat. And that's a sad commentary on the human condition. Wouldn't it be better to save lives than to avenge them? Are we not capable of demonstrating our peaceful intentions by applying all our abilities and our ingenuity to achieving a truly lasting stability? I think we are. Indeed, we must.

After careful consultation with my advisers, including the Joint Chiefs of Staff, I believe there is a way. Let me share with you a vision of the future which offers hope. It is that we embark on a program to counter the awesome Soviet missile threat with measures that are defensive. Let us turn to the very strengths in technology that spawned our great industrial base and that have given us the quality of life we enjoy today.

What if free people could live secure in the knowledge that their security did not rest upon the threat of instant U.S. retaliation to deter a Soviet attack, that we could intercept and destroy strategic ballistic missiles before they reached our own soil or that of our allies?

I know this is a formidable, technical task, one that may not be accomplished before the end of this century. Yet, current technology has attained a level of sophistication where it's reasonable for us to begin this effort. It will take years, probably decades of effort on many fronts. There will be failures and setbacks, just as there will be successes and breakthroughs. And as we proceed, we must remain constant in preserving the nuclear deterrent and

Celluloid button for Reagan.

maintaining a solid capability for flexible response. But isn't it worth every investment necessary to free the world from the threat of nuclear war? We know it is.

In the meantime, we will continue to pursue real reductions in nuclear arms, negotiating from a position of strength that can be ensured only by modernizing our strategic forces. At the same time, we must take steps to reduce the risk of a conventional military conflict escalating to nuclear war by improving our nonnuclear capabilities.

America does possess—now—the technologies to attain very significant improvements in the effectiveness of our conventional, nonnuclear forces. Proceeding boldly with these new techniques, we can significantly reduce any incentive that the Soviet Union may have to threaten attack against the United States or its allies.

As we pursue our goal of defensive technologies, we recognize that our allies rely upon our strategic offensive power to deter attacks against them. Their vital interests and ours are one. And no change in technology can or will alter that reality. We must and shall continue to honor our commitments.

Second Inaugural Address

Ronald
REAGAN
President

Ge
BUS

Inaugural Day 1985 fell on a Sunday. Reagan took the oath of office, as required by the Constitution, at a private ceremony in the White House. The formal inauguration was scheduled for the following day. But on Sunday afternoon, the inaugural committee came to the White House and urged Reagan to cancel the outdoor ceremony because the windchill factor was predicted to be twenty degrees below zero or worse. So, on the twenty-first of January, just before noon, Reagan again took the oath of office before about one thousand people in the Capitol rotunda, and then delivered his second inaugural address.

There are no words adequate to express my thanks for the great honor that you have bestowed on me. I will do my utmost to be deserving of your trust.

This is, as Senator Mathias told us, the 50th time that we the people have celebrated this historic occasion. When the first President, George Washington, placed his hand upon the Bible, he stood less than a single day's journey by horseback from raw, untamed wilderness. There were 4 million Americans in a union of 13 States. Today we are 60 times as many in a union of 50 States. We have lighted the world with our inventions, gone to the aid of mankind wherever in the world there was a cry for help, journeyed to the Moon and safely returned. So much has changed. And yet we stand together as we did two centuries ago.

When I took this oath four years ago, I did so in a time of economic stress. Voices were raised saying we had to look to our past for the greatness and glory. But we, the present-day Americans, are not given to looking backward. In this blessed land, there is always a better tomorrow.

Four years ago, I spoke to you of a new beginning and we have accomplished that. But in another sense, our new beginning is a continuation of that beginning created two centuries ago when, for the first time in history, government, the people said, was not our master, it is our servant; its only power that which we the people allow it to have.

That system has never failed us, but, for a time, we failed the system. We asked things of government that government was not equipped to give. We yielded authority to the National Government that properly belonged to States or to local governments or to the people themselves. We allowed taxes and inflation to rob us of our earnings and savings and watched the great industrial machine that had made us the most productive people on Earth slow down and the number of unemployed increase.

By 1980, we knew it was time to renew our faith, to strive with all our

The Challenger Tragedy

Ronald Reagan's "Great Communicator" reputation rested on his outstanding ability to use television to genuinely touch a mass audience. However much he relied on the precise reading of the words written by his talented speech writers, Reagan's presentation invariably conveyed his emotional belief in a message usually resonating with themes of simple virtue and patriotism. In 1986, when the space shuttle *Challenger* shockingly exploded, killing its seven-person crew, the president rose to the bitter occasion in a nationally televised speech.

Ladies and gentlemen, I'd planned to speak to you tonight about the State of the Union, but the events of earlier today have led me to change those plans. Today is a day for mourning and remembering. Nancy and I are pained to the core by the tragedy of the shuttle *Challenger*. We know we share this pain with all of the people of the country. This is truly a national loss.

Nineteen years ago, almost to the day, we lost three astronauts in a terrible accident on the ground. But we've never lost an astronaut in flight; we've never had a tragedy like this. And perhaps we've forgotten the courage it took for the crew of the shuttle. But they, the *Challenger* Seven, were aware of the dangers, but overcame them and did their jobs brilliantly. We mourn seven heroes: Michael Smith, Dick Scobee, Judith Resnik, Ronald McNair, Ellison Onizuka, Gregory Jarvis, and Christa McAuliffe. We mourn their loss as a nation together.

For the families of the seven, we cannot bear, as you do, the full impact of this tragedy. But we feel the loss, and we're thinking about you so very much. Your loved ones were daring and brave, and they had that special grace, that special spirit that says, "Give me a challenge, and I'll meet it with joy." They had a hunger to explore the universe and discover its truths. They wished to serve, and they did. They served all of us. We've grown used to wonders in this century. It's hard to dazzle us. But for 25 years the United States space program has been doing just that. We've grown used to the idea of space, and perhaps we forget that we've only just begun. We're still pioneers. They, the members of the *Challenger* crew, were pioneers.

I've always had great faith in and respect for our space program, and what happened today does nothing to diminish it. We don't hide our space program. We don't keep secrets and cover things up. We do it all up front and in public. That's the way freedom is, and we wouldn't change it for a minute. We'll continue our quest in space. There will be more shuttle flights and more shuttle crews and, yes, more volunteers, more civilians, more teachers in space. Nothing ends here; our hopes and our journeys continue. I want to add that I wish I could talk to every man and woman who works for NASA or who worked on this mission and tell them: "Your dedication and professionalism have moved and impressed us for decades. And we know of your anguish. We share it."

There's a coincidence today. On this day 390 years ago, the great explorer Sir Francis Drake died aboard ship off the coast of Panama. In his lifetime the great frontiers were the oceans, and an historian later said, "He lived by the sea, died on it, and was buried in it." Well, today we can say of the *Challenger* crew: Their dedication was, like Drake's, complete.

The crew of the space shuttle *Challenger* honored us by the manner in which they lived their lives. We will never forget them, nor the last time we saw them, this morning, as they prepared for their journey and waved good-bye and "slipped the surly bonds of earth" to "touch the face of God." And I want to say something to the schoolchildren of America who were watching the live coverage of the shuttle's takeoff. I know it is hard to understand, but sometimes painful things like this happen. It's all part of the process of exploration and discovery. It's all part of taking a chance and expanding man's horizons. The future doesn't belong to the fainthearted; it belongs to the brave. The *Challenger* crew was pulling us into the future, and we'll continue to follow them.

According to the Gallup Poll, Ronald Reagan ended his second term of office in January 1989 with the highest approval rating of any president since Franklin Roosevelt. Sixty-three percent approved of the job Reagan had done. This compares with the final approval ratings of 58 percent for John Kennedy and 59 percent for Dwight Eisenhower, the presidents who previously had the highest ratings since Roosevelt's 66 percent. In addition, as Reagan's final term drew to a close, public confidence in his leadership returned to the level he enjoyed before the Iran-contra scandal broke. And, unlike his modern predecessors, his final standing with the public is near the high points of his tenure. In contrast, his eight predecessors, as monitored by one half-century of Gallup Polls, finished well below their peaks.

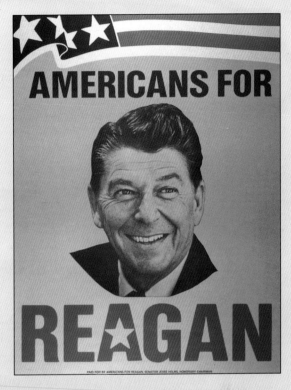

Reagan's political resilience, exemplified by his ability to surmount crises such as the Iran-contra affair, doubtless owed much to his enduring personal appeal. Throughout his tenure, the percentage of Americans approving of Reagan as a person moved in a narrow range, from a low of 67 percent in mid-1983 to a high of 81 percent in late 1985. As he ended his second term, 79 percent approved of him as a person while 13 percent disapproved. Majorities from all walks of life and political persuasions, including those who disapproved of his performance in office, held positive opinions of Reagan, the man.

Reagan's Farewell Address

Reagan left office in 1989 unimpressed by his reputation as the Great Communicator, a phrase often used by his opponents to suggest that Americans liked not what Reagan said but the way he said it. Reagan disagreed, saying that it was the content of his message that attracted people: "I wasn't a great communicator, but I communicated great things, and they didn't spring full bloom from my brow, they came from the heart of a great nation—from our experience, our wisdom, and our belief in the principles that have guided us for two centuries." On January 11, 1989, Ronald Reagan, following in the tradition of Washington, Jackson, and Eisenhower, delivered this Farewell Address to the American people.

My Fellow Americans:

This is the 34th time I'll speak to you from the Oval Office and the last. We've been together eight years now, and soon it'll be time for me to go. But before I do, I wanted to share some thoughts, some of which I've been saving for a long time.

It's been the honor of my life to be your President. So many of you have written the past few weeks to say thanks, but I could say as much to you. Nancy and I are grateful for the opportunity you gave us to serve.

One of the things about the Presidency is that you're always somewhat apart. You spend a lot of time going by too fast in a car someone else is driving, and seeing the people through tinted glass—the parents holding up a child, and the wave you saw too late and couldn't return. And so many times I wanted to stop and reach out from behind the glass, and connect. Well, maybe I can do a little of that tonight.

People ask how I feel about leaving. And the fact is, "parting is such sweet sorrow." The sweet part is California and the ranch and freedom. The sorrow—the goodbyes, of course, and leaving this beautiful place.

You know, down the hall and up the stairs from this office is the part of the White House where the President and his family live. There are a few favorite windows I have up there that I like to stand and look out of early in the morning. The view is over the grounds here to the Washington Monument, and then the Mall and the Jefferson Memorial. But on mornings when the humidity is low, you can see past the Jefferson to the river, the Potomac, and the Virginia shore. Someone said that's the view Lincoln had when he saw the smoke rising from the Battle of Bull Run. I see more prosaic things: the grass on the banks, the morning traffic as people make their way to work, now and then a sailboat on the river.

I've been thinking a bit at that window. I've been reflecting on what the past eight years have meant and mean. And the image that comes to mind like a refrain is a nautical one—a small story about a big ship, and a refugee, and a sailor. It was back in the early eighties, at the height of the boat people. And the sailor was hard at work on the carrier *Midway*, which was patrolling the South China Sea. The sailor, like most American servicemen, was young, smart, and fiercely observant. The crew spied on the horizon a leaky little boat. And crammed inside were refugees from Indochina hoping to get to America. The *Midway* sent a small launch to bring them to the ship and safety. As the refugees made their way through the choppy seas, one spied the sailor on deck, and stood up, and called out to him. He yelled, "Hello, American sailor. Hello, freedom man."

A small moment with a big meaning, a moment the sailor, who wrote it in a letter, couldn't get out of his mind. And, when I saw it, neither could I. Because that's what it was to be an American in the 1980s. We stood, again, for freedom. I know we always have, but in the past few years the world again—and in a way, we ourselves—rediscovered it.

It's been quite a journey this decade, and we held together through some stormy seas. And at the end, together, we are reaching our destination.

The fact is, from Grenada to the Washington and Moscow summits, from the recession of '81 to '82, to the expansion that began in late '82 and continues to this day, we've made a difference. The way I see it, there were two great triumphs, two things that I'm proudest of. One is the economic recovery, in which the people of America created—and filled—19 million new jobs. The other is the recovery of our morale. America is respected again in the world and looked to for leadership.

Something that happened to me a few years ago reflects some of this. It was back in 1981, and I was attending my first big economic summit, which was held that year in Canada. The meeting place rotates among the member countries. The opening meeting was a formal dinner of the heads of government of the seven industrialized nations. Now, I sat there like the new kid in school and listened, and it was all Francois this and Helmut that. They dropped titles and spoke to one another on a first-name basis. Well, at one point I sort of leaned in and said, "My name's Ron." Well, in that same year, we began the actions we felt would ignite an economic comeback—cut taxes and regulation, started to cut spending. And soon the recovery began.

Two years later, another economic summit with pretty much the same cast. At the big opening meeting we all got together, and all of a sudden, just for a moment, I saw that everyone was just sitting there looking at me. And then one of them broke the silence. "Tell us about the American miracle," he said.

Well, back in 1980, when I was running for President, it was all so different. Some pundits said our programs would result in catastrophe. Our views on foreign affairs would cause war. Our plans for the economy would cause inflation to soar and bring about economic collapse. I even remember one highly respected economist saying, back in 1982, that "The engines of economic growth have shut down here, and they're likely to stay that way for years to come." Well, he and the other opinion leaders were wrong. The fact is what they call "radical" was really "right." What they called "dangerous" was just "desperately needed."

And in all of that time I won a nickname, "The Great Communicator." But I never though it was my style or the words I used that made a difference: it was the content. I wasn't a great communicator, but I communicated great things, and they didn't spring full bloom from my brow, they came from the heart of a great nation—from our experience, our wisdom, and our belief in the principles that have guided us for two centuries. They called it the Reagan revolution. Well, I'll accept that, but for me it always seemed more like the great rediscovery, a rediscovery of our values and our common sense.

Common sense told us that when you put a big tax on something, the people will produce less of it. So, we cut the people's tax rates, and the people produced more than ever before. The economy bloomed like a plant that had been cut back and could now grow quicker and stronger. Our economic program brought about the longest peacetime expansion in our history: real family income up, the poverty rate down, entrepreneurship booming, and an explosion in research and new technology. We're exporting more than ever because American industry because more competitive and at the same time, we summoned the national will to knock down protectionist walls abroad instead of erecting them at home.

Common sense also told us that to preserve the peace, we'd have to become strong again after years of weakness and confusion. So, we rebuilt our defenses, and this New Year we toasted the new peacefulness around the globe. Not only have the superpowers actually begun to reduce their stockpiles of nuclear weapons—and hope for even more progress is bright—but the regional conflicts that rack the globe are also beginning to cease. The Persian Gulf is no longer a war zone. The Soviets are leaving Afghanistan. The Vietnamese are preparing to pull out of Cambodia, and an American-mediated accord will soon send 50,000 Cuban troops home from Angola.

The lesson of all this was, of course, that because we're a great nation, our challenges seem complex. It will always be this way. But as long as we remember our first principles and believe in ourselves, the future will always be ours. And something else we learned: Once you begin a great movement, there's no telling where it will end. We meant to change a nation, and instead, we changed a world.

Countries across the globe are turning to free markets and free speech and turning away from the ideologies of the past. For them, the great rediscovery of the 1980s has been that, lo and behold, the moral way of government is the practical way of government: Democracy, the profoundly good, is also the profoundly productive.

When you've got to the point when you can celebrate the anniversaries of your 39th birthday you can sit back sometimes, review your life, and see it flowing before you. For me there was a fork in the river, and it was right in the middle of my life. I never meant to go into politics. It wasn't my intention when

I was young. But I was raised to believe you had to pay your way for the blessings bestowed on you. I was happy with my career in the entertainment world, but I ultimately went into politics because I wanted to protect something precious.

Ours was the first revolution in the history of mankind that truly reversed the course of government, and with three little words: "We the People." "We the People" tell the government what to do; it doesn't tell us. "We the People" are the driver; the government is the car. And we decide where it should go, and by what route, and how fast. Almost all the world's constitutions are documents in which governments tell the people what their privileges are. Our Constitution is a document in which "We the People" tell the government what it is allowed to do. "We the People" are free. This belief has been the underlying basis for everything I've tried to do these past eight years.

But back in the 1960s, when I began, it seemed to me that we'd begun reversing the order of things—that through more and more rules and regulations and confiscatory taxes, the government was taking more of our money, more of our options, and more of our freedom. I went into politics in part to put up my hand and say, "Stop." I was a citizen politician, and it seemed the right thing for a citizen to do.

I think we have stopped a lot of what needed stopping. And I hope we have once again reminded people that man is not free unless government is limited. There's a clear cause and effect here that is as neat and predictable as a law of physics: As government expands, liberty contracts.

Nothing is less free than pure communism—and yet we have, the past few years, forged a satisfying new closeness with the Soviet Union. I've been asked if this isn't a gamble, and my answer is no because we're basing our actions not on words but deeds. The *detente* of the 1970s was based not on actions but promises. They'd promise to treat their own people and the people of the world better. But the *gulag* was still the *gulag*, and the state was still expansionist, and they still waged proxy wars in Africa, Asia, and Latin America.

Well, this time, so far, it's different. President Gorbachev has brought about some internal democratic reforms and begun the withdrawal from Afghanistan. He has also freed prisoners whose names I've given him every time we've met.

But life has a way of reminding you of big things through small incidents. Once, during the heady days of the Moscow summit, Nancy and I decided to break off from the entourage one afternoon to visit the shops on Arbat Street—that's a little street just off Moscow's main shopping area. Even though our visit was a surprise, every Russian there immediately recognized us and called out our names and reached for our hands. We were just about swept away by the warmth. You could almost feel the possibilities in all that joy. But within seconds, a KGB detail pushed their way toward us and began pushing and shoving the people in the crowd. It was an interesting moment. It reminded me that while the man on the street in the Soviet Union yearns for peace, the government is Communist. And those who run it are Communists, and that means we and they view such issues as freedom and human rights very differently.

We must keep up our guard, but we must also continue to work together to lessen and eliminate tension and mistrust. My view is that President Gorbachev is different from previous Soviet leaders. I think he knows some of the things wrong with his society and is trying to fix them. We wish him well. And we'll continue to work to make sure that the Soviet Union that eventually emerges from this process is a less threatening one. What it all boils down to is this: I want the new closeness to continue. And it will, as long as we make it clear that we will continue to act in a certain way as long as they continue to act in a helpful manner. If and when they don't, at first pull your punches. If they persist, pull the plug. It's still trust by verify. It's still play, but cut the cards. It's still watch closely. And don't be afraid to see what you see.

I've been asked if I have any regrets. Well, I do. The deficit is one. I've been talking a great deal about that lately, but tonight isn't for arguments, and I'm

How much credit is due President Reagan for bringing Soviet leader Mikhail Gorbachev to the nuclear bargaining table remains a matter of debate. However, unlike some who shared his anti-Soviet views, Reagan also made it clear that he advocated a military buildup as a means toward the goal of arms reduction. The turnaround in U.S.-Soviet relations in the final two years of the Reagan presidency is perhaps his most enduring legacy. This turnaround was a prelude to the dissolution of the Soviet Union (1990) and to far-reaching arms reduction agreements made by the ensuing Bush administration.

going to hold my tongue. But an observation: I've had my share of victories in the Congress, but what few people noticed is that I never won anything you didn't win for me. They never saw my troops, they never saw Reagan's regiments, the American people. You won every battle with every call you made and letter you wrote demanding action. Well, action is still needed if we're to finish the job. Reagan's regiments will have to become the Bush brigades. Soon he'll be the chief, and he'll need you every bit as much as I did.

Finally, there is a great tradition of warnings in Presidential farewells, and I've got one that's been on my mind for some time. But oddly enough it starts with one of the things I'm proudest of in the past eight years: the resurgence of national pride that I called the new patriotism. This national feeling is good, but it won't count for much, and it won't last unless it's grounded in thoughtfulness and knowledge.

An informed patriotism is what we want. And are we doing a good enough job teaching our children what America is and what she represents in the long history of the world? Those of us who are over 35 or so years of age grew up in a different America. We were taught, very directly, what it means to be an

American. And we absorbed, almost in the air, a love of country and an appreciation of its institutions. If you didn't get these things from your family you got them from the neighborhood, from the father down the street who fought in Korea or the family who lost someone at Anzio. Or you could get a sense of patriotism from school. And if all else failed you could get a sense of patriotism from the popular culture. The movies celebrated democratic values and implicitly reinforced the idea that America was special. TV was like that, too, through the mid-sixties.

But now, we're about to enter the nineties, and some things have changed. Younger parents aren't sure that an unambivalent appreciation of America is the right thing to teach modern children. And as for those who create the popular culture, well-grounded patriotism is no longer the style. Our spirit is back, but we haven't reinstitutionalized it. We've got to do a better job of getting across that America is freedom—freedom of speech, freedom of religion, freedom of enterprise. And freedom is special and rare. It's fragile; it needs protection.

So, we've got to teach history based not on what's in fashion but what's important—why the Pilgrims came here, who Jimmy Doolittle was, and what those 30 seconds over Tokyo meant. You know, four years ago on the 40th anniversary of D-day, I read a letter from a young woman writing to her late father, who'd fought on Omaha Beach. Her name was Lisa Zanatta Henn, and she said, "we will always remember, we will never forget what the boys of Normandy did." Well, let's help her keep her word. If we forget what we did, we won't know who we are. I'm warning of an eradication of the American memory that could result, ultimately, in an erosion of the American spirit. Let's start with some basics: more attention to American history and a greater emphasis on civic ritual.

And let me offer lesson number one about America: All great change in America begins at the dinner table. So, tomorrow night in the kitchen I hope the talking begins. And children, if your parents haven't been teaching you what it means to be an American, let 'em know and nail 'em on it. That would be a very American thing to do.

And that's about all I have to say tonight, except for one thing. The past few days when I've been at that window upstairs, I've thought a bit of the "shining city upon a hill." The phrase comes from John Winthrop, who wrote it to describe the America he imagined. What he imagined was important because he was an early Pilgrim, an early freedom man. He journeyed here on what today we'd call a little wooden boat; and like the other Pilgrims, he was looking for a home that would be free. I've spoken of the shining city all my political life, but I don't know if I ever quite communicated what I saw when I said it. But in my mind it was a tall, proud city built on rocks stronger than oceans, windswept, God-blessed, and teeming with people of all kinds living in harmony and peace; a city with free ports that hummed with commerce and creativity. And if there had to be city walls, the walls had doors and the doors were open to anyone with the will and the heart to get here. That's how I saw it, and see it still.

And how stands the city on this winter night? More prosperous, more secure, and happier than it was eight years ago. But more than that: After 200 years, two centuries, she still stands strong and true on the granite ridge, and her glow has held steady no matter what storm. And she's still a beacon, still a magnet for all who must have freedom, for all the pilgrims from all the lost places who are hurtling through the darkness, toward home.

We've done our part. And as I walk off into the city streets, a final word to the men and women of the Reagan revolution, the men and women across America who for eight years did the work that brought America back. My friends: We did it. We weren't just marking time. We made a difference. We made the city stronger, we made the city freer, and we left her in good hands. All in all, not bad, not bad at all.

And so, goodbye, God bless you, and God bless the United States of America.

Further Reading

GENERAL REFERENCE

Israel, Fred L. *Student's Atlas of American Presidential Elections, 1789–1996*. Washington, D.C.: Congressional Quarterly Books, 1998.

Levy, Peter B., editor. *100 Key Documents in American History*. Westport, Conn.: Praeger, 1999.

Mieczkowski, Yarek. *The Routledge Historical Atlas of Presidential Elections*. New York: Routledge, 2001.

Polsby, Nelson W., and Aaron Wildavsky. *Presidential Elections: Strategies and Structures of American Politics*. 10th edition. New York: Chatham House, 2000.

Watts, J. F., and Fred L. Israel, editors. *Presidential Documents*. New York: Routledge, 2000.

Widmer, Ted. *The New York Times Campaigns: A Century of Presidential Races*. New York: DK Publishing, 2000.

POLITICAL AMERICANA REFERENCE

Cunningham, Noble E. Jr. *Popular Images of the Presidency: From Washington to Lincoln*. Columbia: University of Missouri Press, 1991.

Melder, Keith. *Hail to the Candidate: Presidential Campaigns from Banners to Broadcasts*. Washington, D.C.: Smithsonian Institution Press, 1992.

Schlesinger, Arthur M. jr., Fred L. Israel, and David J. Frent. *Running for President: The Candidates and their Images*. 2 vols. New York: Simon and Schuster, 1994.

Warda, Mark. *100 Years of Political Campaign Collectibles*. Clearwater, Fla.: Galt Press, 1996.

THE ELECTION OF 1980
And the Administration of Ronald Reagan

Boyer, Paul, editor. *Reagan as President: Contemporary Views of the Man, His Politics, and his Policies*. Chicago: Ivan R. Dee, 2002.

Carter, Jimmy. *Keeping Faith: Memoirs of a President*. New York: Bantam Doubleday Dell, 1982.

Dallek, Matthew. *The Right Moment: Ronald Reagan's First Victory and the Decisive Turning Point in American Politics*. New York: Free Press, 2000.

D'Souza, Dinesh. Ronald Reagan: *How an Ordinary Man Became an Extraordinary Leader*. Carmichael, Calif.: Touchstone Books, 1999.

Fitzgerald, Frances. *Way Out There in the Blue: Reagan and Star Wars and the End of the Cold War*. New York: Simon and Schuster, 2000.

Germond, Jack. *Blue Smoke and Mirrors: How Reagan Won and Why Carter Lost the Election of 1980*. New York: Viking Press, 1981.

Grover, William F. *The President as Prisoner: A Structural Critique of the Carter and Reagan Years*. Albany: State University of New York Press, 1989.

Morris, Edmund. *Dutch: A Memoir of Ronald Reagan*. New York: Random House, 1999.

Noonan, Peggy. *When Character Was King: A Story of Ronald Reagan*. New York: Viking Press, 2001

Reagan, Ronald. *An American Life*. New York: Simon & Schuster, 1990.

Stacks, John F. *Watershed: The Campaign for the Presidency 1980*. New York: Times Books, 1981.

INDEX

Numbers in **bold italics** refer to captions.

The EDITORS

ARTHUR M. SCHLESINGER JR. holds the Albert Schweitzer Chair in the Humanities at the Graduate Center of the City University of New York. He is the author of more than a dozen books, including *The Age of Jackson*; *The Vital Center; The Age of Roosevelt* (3 vols.); *A Thousand Days: John F. Kennedy in the White House; Robert Kennedy and His Times; The Cycles of American History;* and *The Imperial Presidency.* Professor Schlesinger served as Special Assistant to President Kennedy (1961–63). His numerous awards include: the Pulitzer Prize for History; the Pulitzer Prize for Biography; two National Book Awards; The Bancroft Prize; and the American Academy of Arts and Letters Gold Medal for History.

FRED L. ISRAEL is professor emeritus of American history, City College of New York. He is the author of *Nevada's Key Pittman* and has edited *The War Diary of Breckinridge Long* and *Major Peace Treaties of Modern History, 1648–1975* (5 vols.) He holds the Scribe's Award from the American Bar Association for his joint editorship of the *Justices of the United States Supreme Court* (4 vols.). For more than 25 years Professor Israel has compiled and edited the Gallup Poll into annual reference volumes.

DAVID J. FRENT is the president of Political Americana Auctions, Oakhurst, NJ. With his wife, Janice, he has assembled the nation's foremost private collection of political campaign memorabilia. Mr. Frent has designed exhibits for corporations, the Smithsonian Institution, and the United States Information Agency. A member of the board of directors of the American Political Items Collectors since 1972, he was elected to its Hall of Fame for his "outstanding contribution to preserving and studying our political heritage."